Rooms with
a View

Also by Adrian Mourby

Rooms of One's Own: 50 Places That Made Literary History

Rooms with a View

The Secret Life of Grand Hotels

ADRIAN MOURBY

Published in the UK in 2017 by
Icon Books Ltd, Omnibus Business Centre,
39–41 North Road, London N7 9DP
email: info@iconbooks.com
www.iconbooks.com

Sold in the UK, Europe and Asia
by Faber & Faber Ltd, Bloomsbury House,
74–77 Great Russell Street,
London WC1B 3DA or their agents

Distributed in the UK, Europe and Asia
by TBS Ltd, TBS Distribution Centre, Colchester Road,
Frating Green, Colchester CO7 7DW

Distributed in the USA by
Publishers Group West,
1700 Fourth Street, Berkeley, CA 94710

Distributed in Canada by Publishers Group Canada,
76 Stafford Street, Unit 300,
Toronto, Ontario M6J 2S1

Distributed in Australia and New Zealand
by Allen & Unwin Pty Ltd,
PO Box 8500, 83 Alexander Street,
Crows Nest, NSW 2065

Distributed in South Africa by
Jonathan Ball, Office B4, The District,
41 Sir Lowry Road, Woodstock 7925

ISBN: 978-178578-275-6

Typesetting by Simmons Pugh

Printed and bound in the UK by Clays Ltd, St Ives plc

To my mother
Margaret 'Peggy' Mourby
who loved a good hotel

Adrian Mourby was an award-winning BBC drama producer before turning to full-time writing. He has published three novels, two AA travel guides and a book of humour based on his Sony Award-winning Radio 4 series *Whatever Happened To...?* He is also the author of *Rooms of One's Own: 50 Places That Made Literary History* (Icon, 2017). In recent years Adrian has won two Italian awards for his travel journalism. He writes extensively on opera, has produced works by Mozart, Handel and Purcell and leads cultural tours worldwide.

CONTENTS

INTRODUCTION   11

THE AMERICAS

Parker House Hotel, Boston   18

Hotel Monteleone, New Orleans   23

Le Château Frontenac, Québec City   28

The Algonquin, New York   33

Plaza Hotel, New York   38

Copacabana Palace, Rio de Janeiro   43

Royal Hawaiian, Waikiki   48

Biltmore Hotel, Miami   54

UNITED KINGDOM

The Langham, London   59

The Randolph, Oxford   64

The Savoy, London   68

The Caledonian, Edinburgh   74

The Waldorf, London   79

The Dorchester, London   84

The Midland Hotel, Morecambe   90

FRANCE

Le Meurice, Paris   96
Grand Hotel Terminus, Paris   101
The Ritz, Paris   106
The Carlton Hotel, Cannes   112

GERMANY

Frankfurter Hof, Frankfurt   118
The Adlon Hotel, Berlin   123

AUSTRIA

Imperial Hotel, Vienna   130
Hotel Sacher, Vienna   135

SWITZERLAND

Hotel des Bergues, Geneva   141
Baur au Lac, Zurich   146
Gstaad Palace, Gstaad   152

ITALY

Hôtel de Russie, Rome   157
The Gritti Palace, Venice   162
Londra Palace, Venice   167
Grand Hotel et de Milan, Milan   171
Hotel Eden, Rome   176

Grand Hotel Tremezzo, Lake Como   181
Hotel Cipriani, Venice   186

GREECE
Hotel Grande Bretagne, Athens   192

POLAND
Hotel Bristol, Warsaw   198

RUSSIA
Grand Hotel d'Europe, St Petersburg   204
Hotel Astoria, St Petersburg   209

TURKEY
Pera Palace Hotel, Istanbul   215

AFRICA
Mena House, Giza, Egypt   221
Reid's New Hotel, Funchal, Madeira   226
Hotel de la Mamounia Transatlantique et CFM,
Marrakech, Morocco   231
Hotel Cecil, Alexandria, Egypt   237

INDIA
Taj Mahal Hotel, Bombay   242

The Imperial Hotel, Delhi   247

ASIA

The Oriental Hotel, Bangkok, Thailand   252

The Continental Hotel, Saigon, Vietnam   257

Raffles Hotel, Singapore   262

Le Métropole, Hanoi, Vietnam   267

The Cathay Hotel, Shanghai, China   272

The Peninsula, Hong Kong, China   277

A PERSONAL NOTE   284

ACKNOWLEDGEMENTS   287

GUEST LIST   290

BEHIND THE SCENES   299

NOTE

*Hotels have always changed their names on a frequent basis and continue to do so. In the
contents above I have given the name by which a hotel was first known, or its most common
name over the years. At the top of each chapter, however, I also give the most recent name of
those hotels that are continuing to reinvent or rebrand themselves.*

*In each of the fourteen sections hotels are arranged in chronological order rather than by
country as the timeline tells a better story.*

INTRODUCTION

Each grand hotel has its own story. It might be the life of the remarkable person who built or ran it, or the people who designed it, or the famous people who have stayed there. Sometimes it's the story of events – usually wars and revolutions – that happened around the hotel and even inside.

In this book I set out to tell the unique stories of 50 different grand hotels that can still be visited today. I like them all; I hope you will too.

Over many years of travelling I've tried to discover what makes each grand hotel the place it is. It would have been far too easy to write about 50 hotels where Hemingway drank, Noël Coward quipped, Churchill smoked, Josephine Baker danced in very few clothes, and Marlene Dietrich was paid a small fortune to mumble into a microphone.

Stories like those can be heard all round the world. They are beguiling hotel gossip – and hotels are as full of gossip, myths and ghosts as theatres. I've tried to weigh these anecdotes and only report on those that can be substantiated. Many cannot. Hotels and hyperbole have long gone hand in hand.

Inevitably a book like this poses the question: What actually is a grand hotel?

Although the first hotel to call itself 'grand' in the English language opened in London's Covent Garden in 1774, the grand hotel is a nineteenth-century concept. The aspiration to grandeur allowed the commercial hotel to become respectable – and then positively regal.

In this book you will read about the visionaries who transformed the city hotel from a dowdy refuge for those who lacked a townhouse of their own – or friends and family nearby – to a residence that exceeded even the expectations of royalty. Many hotels in this book were where kings and aristocrats chose to live or accommodate their visitors because their own apartments could not compete with such levels of comfort and service.

In a short space of time in the second half of the nineteenth century the idea of hotels as a lifestyle choice – rather than a necessity – took root. Not all existing hotels, in fact very few, made that transformation. Many new hotels were built to that purpose but failed. However, those that did achieve grandeur were able to offer a wholly different perspective on the world. The only contemporary parallel to this phenomenon that I can suggest is if a few overambitious monomaniacs today decided that the airport terminal was no longer going to be a function of travel but become a place so comfortable and with such exemplary levels of service we would all aspire to live in it. That was the ambition of the men – and occasionally women – who pioneered the grand hotel concept across the world.

In writing this book I've found that grand hotels begin life in varied circumstances but end up – if they survive – leading very similar lives today. Their exciting stories lie at the end of the nineteenth century and in the early decades of the twentieth century when extravagant deeds were done and great challenges overcome. Setbacks at this time took the form of natural disasters, fires and floods, bankruptcies and revolutions, plus major political upheavals and the First World War. The hotels that are with us today survived such dramatic disruptions.

Then in the interwar years most grand hotels became lucrative and glamorous havens from the financial crashes and the rise of totalitarianism. Politicians, heads of state, movie stars, and celebrity writers flocked to them. Often Edward, the playboy Prince of Wales, put in an appearance (with or without Mrs Simpson), Josephine Baker danced and Hemingway drank at the bar.

But then came the Second World War. Although the Great War (1914–18) had some impact on some hotels, its sequel (1939–45) affected just about *every* grand hotel in the world, even in the Americas, where Miami's glamorous Biltmore was turned into a hospital and couples were arrested in front of the Copacabana Palace for indecency during the blackout. During the Second World War people partied all night at grand hotels as if there were no tomorrow (sometimes there wasn't). As Europe and Asia went up in flames, hotels were bombed out or disappeared behind sandbags and barbed wire. During this time many hotels played host to the major protagonists, everyone from Winston Churchill to Hitler, from Eisenhower to Rommel, and all the writers and artists who covered the war.

What happened to those grand hotels that survived depended on which side of the Iron Curtain the property found itself. The process of recovery in Eastern Europe lagged behind the West by a good 40 years. Under Communism in Europe and Asia, grand hotels fared as badly as the human populations whose lives were blighted by these regimes.

But then the drama fades – it evaporates – and for the best reasons. Those grand hotels that were not demolished or modernised beyond recognition in the period post-1945 entered upon a time of gradual recovery. There were some embarrassingly gaudy flirtations with 1960s makeovers and lowered ceilings, but eventually we all learned lessons about respecting the authenticity of historic buildings. For the grand hotel this was the era of the jet-set, with Richard Burton and Elizabeth Taylor passing through, with Danny Kaye, Roger

Moore, Zsa Zsa Gabor, Joan Collins, and a handful of minor royals in their wake. Hotel archives, sparse indeed when covering the early days, now become crammed with fading colour photographs of forgotten general managers standing next to celebrities no one can remember at all.

Then in the 1980s and 90s those grand hotels that survived intact were rediscovered for their unique qualities, often returning to the vision of the nineteenth-century pioneers who brought them into existence.

It takes a huge amount of money to build a truly great hotel and it takes pretty much the same amount periodically to maintain it. We have to be grateful therefore that there are people in this world who pour their profits into supporting these grand hotels. Their reasons for doing so may be financial, vainglorious or even sentimental, but thank goodness they do. Maybe they simply love grand hotels.

All the hotels in *Rooms with a View* are very successful now. Many of them are much-loved national and international institutions. My interest lies in the drama of their earlier days, however, because that is where their individuality was forged. Fortunately hotels no longer live in 'interesting' times. They live in wonderful times. Never have our grand hotels looked so good. Never has so much money been pumped into them nor have they been so popular with visitors.

It goes without saying that I have visited all the hotels featured in this book because I wanted to write about ones that still function as hotels today. Unfortunately this meant excluding several great hotels which at the time of writing were undergoing lengthy refurbishments. All the hotels in this book – bar one – have been very cooperative in helping me with my research. A few, however, would rather their myths go uninvestigated.

Sadly, many of the world's greatest monuments to hospitality have not survived. So I'd like to take a moment to remember the many grand hotels that were lost in the twentieth century, lost to bombs and to debts and to the simple arrogance of architects and destructive developers who thought they knew better.

After the Second World War, the Carlton in London was demolished to make way for the loathsome New Zealand House, one of the most acontextual buildings in a beautiful city. The Grand Hôtel du Louvre in Paris was first turned into a shopping mall and then eviscerated when an RAF plane crashed on it in 1943. The Hotel Kaiserhof in Berlin, which burned down within days of opening in 1875, burned down again for good during the Second World War. Frank Lloyd Wright's Imperial Hotel in Tokyo was demolished in 1967 following earthquakes. The Belmont in New York, the tallest building in the world when it opened in 1908, was torn down in 1939 to build the low-rise Art Deco Airlines Building (which in turn was demolished in 1977).

I would love to have visited all those hotels and many more like them. This book is not a lament, however. It is a celebration and a thank you letter to the lovely, crazy people out there who restore grand hotels and keep them going regardless of the cost. And there is so much to celebrate because the grand hotel is one of the great achievements of the nineteenth century which – despite the destructive tendencies of the twentieth – went on to achieve its apotheosis today.

We may live in difficult times but our grand hotels have never been grander.

Adrian Mourby, 2017

ROOMS WITH A VIEW

THE AMERICAS

PARKER HOUSE HOTEL, BOSTON (1855)
OMNI PARKER HOUSE

The Parker House Hotel we see today is a polished granite Neoclassical building that would border on the severe were it not for some Art Deco flourishes and a gaudy showbiz awning of lightbulbs. It wouldn't look out of place in Gershwin's Manhattan. Inside, however, it seems older, having retained some of the detail from the original 1855 hotel opened here by Harvey D. Parker. As a nineteen-year-old farm boy looking to make his fortune, Parker arrived in Boston from Maine in 1825 with very little money but a huge amount of ambition – and great attention to detail. He died a millionaire in 1884.

The first Parker House was a five-storey hotel occupying the same site just off Boston Common. It stood squarely opposite the old City Hall and close to the stately, seventeenth-century King's Chapel. Hotels were not necessarily respectable places in the 1850s but Mr Parker offered his guests many gentlemanly innovations, including what became known as the European Plan for meals. From earliest times US hotels had included all meals in the cost of a room, and only provided them at set times. Parker House was one of the first to charge only for the room, with meals billed as extra and provided whenever the guest wanted them.

Mr Parker worked himself and his staff hard and the hotel quickly became popular with politicians, lawyers and

Photo: Kimberly Vardeman

businessmen who frequented Tremont Street. In the 1860s Parker had to repeatedly expand his hotel, both horizontally and vertically, to keep pace with demand. In 1884, the year of Harvey Parker's death, the façade was given a Neo-Gothic makeover. In 1927 it was reworked again and raised to fourteen towering floors.

Because of its historic location, excellent food and uncommon levels of comfort, Parker House became a noted meeting place, especially for writers, who have always had a particular affinity with the best hotels. Longfellow first read out his poem *Paul Revere's Ride* here in 1860 and Dickens gave a reading of *A Christmas Carol* in the hotel in 1867. The audience on both occasions was the Saturday Club which consisted – among other American literati – of Ralph Waldo Emerson, Nathaniel Hawthorne, Henry James Snr, Longfellow himself, and Oliver Wendell Holmes Snr. These gentlemen met for dinner on the fourth Saturday of every month, except during July, August and September. Their meetings at Parker House led to the setting up of the *Atlantic Monthly* magazine (still published today as *The Atlantic* but now edited in Washington).

Dickens based himself at the hotel for much of his five-month second American tour which ran from December 1867 to April 1868. Jacques Offenbach also stayed at the hotel during his 1876 New England tour. He claimed to have come up with a tune – later used in his final operetta *Tales of Hoffmann* – that was inspired by the famously soft Parker House rolls. The following year Mark Twain was interviewed in his bedroom at Parker House, and told the reporter: 'You see for yourself that I'm pretty near heaven – not theologically, of course, but by the hotel standard.'

One guest of whom the hotel is less proud was John Wilkes Booth, who stayed at the Parker House ten days before assassinating Abraham Lincoln in 1865. Unfortunately no one thought it remarkable that Booth spent so much time practising shooting with pistols during his time at the hotel.

In the following century two members of the Parker House staff would go on to have an even bigger influence on American politics. Ho Chi Minh maintained that he worked at the hotel as a pastry chef in 1912 and Malcolm X (then known as Malcolm Little) worked as a busboy, refilling water glasses in the 1940s. Also in the 1940s John F. Kennedy announced his candidacy for congress at Parker House, and in 1953 he staged his bachelor party here before marrying Jaqueline Bouvier.

As North America's longest-running commercial hotel, the Parker House has had far more than its fair share of history, but it has retained surprisingly few artefacts to show for it. One exception is on the mezzanine, not far from the old Victorian reading library (now Parker's Bar) where a corridor ends abruptly, blocked by a desk and a huge mirror. A plaque nearby records that it was in front of this mirror that Charles Dickens rehearsed during his second American reading tour. This tour earned him over £19,000, a colossal sum for the time and more than he was bringing in from his published works.

Not surprisingly, a building about which so many tales have been told has also found its way into fiction. In Edith Wharton's *The Age of Innocence* (1920) Newland Archer is in Newport, Rhode Island when he learns that the woman he has fallen in love with, Countess Ellen Olenska, is staying at Parker House. Newland rushes off to see her, an event that nearly destroys his marriage.

In 1969 Parker House was acquired by the Dunfey family, who later purchased Omni Hotels and Resorts. They renamed their Boston property Omni Parker as the flagship of the group. It is sometimes said, however, that Harvey Parker never entirely relinquished his hotel. On the tenth floor the ghost of an old man with a black moustache has been seen by guests and staff, answering to the description of Parker. A perfectionist when it came to his hotel, it makes sense that Mr Parker still hasn't entirely left the premises.

PARKER FOOD

The hotel's historic restaurant, now known as Parker's, is a dark-panelled room on the ground floor with low lighting and the ambience of a gentleman's club. In his memoir, *Notes of a Son and Brother* (1914), Henry James recalled how much he enjoyed eating there while a student at Harvard Law School.

A number of famous Boston dishes have their origins in Parker's, not only the folded Parker House roll, coated in melted butter and salt and much beloved of Offenbach, but the chocolate-coated Boston cream pie, created in 1856 and officially the state dessert of Massachusetts.

The restaurant also coined the word 'scrod' for its fish menu. Scrod is not a kind of fish, but a Boston term for the freshest white fish of the day. Its derivation is mysterious, and may be an abbreviation of 'sacred cod'.

HOTEL MONTELEONE, NEW ORLEANS (1886)

With its imposing Beaux-Arts lines, the Monteleone looks like a piece of New York hotel real estate towering over this most European of US cities on the banks of the Mississippi.

The hotel was founded by Antonio Monteleone, an Italian immigrant shoemaker whose family still owns this 600-bedroom block in the French Quarter. In 1880 Antonio sold his shoe factory in Sicily and made his way to New Orleans, joining his uncle in working as a cobbler on Royal Street. From these humble beginnings he had by 1886 earned enough money to buy a 64-room hotel on the corner of Royal and Iberville streets (currently the site of the hotel's Carousel Bar).

Like so many hoteliers Antonio was hugely ambitious. Soon he was merging his small hotel with the nearby Commercial Hotel, under whose name both buildings traded until 1908. That year the hotel expanded to a massive 400 rooms at a cost of $260,000. Antonio brought in the New Orleans architects Albert Toledano and Victor Wogan to completely rebuild what had become known locally as the Monteleone. To crown this achievement Antonio angled a giant illuminated neon sign on the rooftop, with the hotel's name emblazoned in red. It can still be seen there today.

Part of the hotel's early success lay in old Antonio's cheap room rates. He had a policy of always having some rooms available for one dollar a night. Antonio was also benevolent towards his staff and encouraged unionised labour. He created a loyal workforce. Even today, employees have long careers at the Monteleone.

In 1913 after Antonio's death, his son Frank took over and modernised the Monteleone. By 1926 there were radios

HOTEL MONTELEONE, NEW ORLEANS

Photo: © Kate Tadman-Mourby

24

and electric ceiling fans in each of the bedrooms, and air conditioning in the lobby, although he didn't move Antonio's grandfather clock, which has always stood in the lobby, and is still in situ today.

The Monteleone did sufficiently good business in the 1920s and 30s to be able to stay open following the stock market crash of 1929 which closed most of New Orleans's hotels.

Over the years the hotel has always passed from father to son, from Frank to Bill in 1958, and from Bill to William Junior in 2011. These days, with its ballrooms, cocktail lounges, sky terrace and swimming pools, the Monteleone is a byword for luxury in a city that brought loucheness to the United States. But it is the Monteleone's literary connections over the decades that make its story so worth telling.

At the last count there are at least 173 novels and short stories of significance that are set in some way or other at the Monteleone. In June 1999, the hotel was designated an official literary landmark by the Friends of the Library Association, an honour it shares with only two other hotels, the Plaza and Algonquin, both in New York.

Among the literary greats now commemorated in the hotel's five celebrity suites is Truman Capote, who was a regular visitor and who claimed that in 1924 he was born at the Monteleone. Lillie Mae, Truman's mother, was indeed a guest at the hotel when she went into labour, but she was rushed to Touro Hospital in time. Tennessee Williams also wasn't born at the Monteleone but, as a child in Columbus, Mississippi, he used to visit his beloved grandfather, Reverend Walter Dakin, at the Monteleone. Tennessee (who also has a suite named after him) later trumped Truman by claiming to have been conceived at the hotel. He subsequently included references to it in two of his plays, *The Rose Tattoo* (1951) and *Orpheus Descending* (1957).

Another suite commemorates William Faulkner, who in

1929 spent his honeymoon at the hotel – it being the only one open at the time because of the financial crash. A fourth commemorates the ubiquitous Ernest Hemingway who was a frequent visitor with his second wife Pauline when they had a home in Florida during the 1930s. On one occasion in 1937 the Hemingways arrived at the Monteleone with his sons and Pauline's sister for what was described as a 'week of heavy partying'. In 1938 Hemingway wrote a short story about the Spanish Civil War, *Night Before Battle*, in which his fictional cameraman and tank commander recall drinking at the hotel. Sherwood Anderson, Eudora Welty and John Grisham have also stayed here, and the Louisiana authors Anne Rice and Rebecca Wells have referenced the hotel in their fiction.

Not all writers have been happily associated with the Monteleone. In 1942 New Orleans-born author Innis Patterson Truman jumped to her death from the twelfth floor, adding herself to the numerous ghosts who are said to congregate on the hotel's thirteenth floor, which – despite being cautiously designated the fourteenth – has had an unusual amount of paranormal activity reported.

By the 1950s the hotel was showing its age. Mary, the fourth Mrs Hemingway, wrote in 1953 that she and her husband were 'staying at a hotel of frayed glories in Royal Street'. The following year Antonio's son, Frank Monteleone, rebuilt much of his hotel while preserving special features like the gaudy Carousel Bar.

This 25-seater merry-go-round for alcoholics and bon viveurs was installed in 1949 and rotates on 2,000 large steel rollers. It is pulled almost imperceptibly by a chain powered by a one-quarter horsepower engine, completing its 360-degree revolution every fifteen minutes. Patrons sit on painted seats and the canopy of the bar is straight out of a fairground. In the 1950s Tennessee Williams once spent two weeks at the hotel, listening to conversations at the bar which he claimed gave him material for his plays. Apparently Frank Monteleone picked up the monumental tab as a thank you to Williams for bringing New Orleans and Hotel Monteleone worldwide attention.

Why the Monteleone is so popular with writers is difficult to define but that kind of gesture definitely helps.

EUDORA WELTY

The Pulitzer-Prize winning writer Eudora Welty (1909–2001) featured the Monteleone in her short story 'A Curtain of Green' and claimed to have written 'The Purple Hat' while sitting in its Carousel Bar. She stayed at the hotel a number of times. One early visit was in her late twenties in the company of an old college classmate, Migs Schmerhorn. In order to save money the pair gave up their en suite room, 'changing to a cheaper room with the privilege of using the ladies room down hall'.

A sports team were staying with their coach in the next-door room. 'And when we would take a bath they would look over the partition and comment. We reported them in huffy manner and [a] house dick was sent up to sit down hall with grey fedora over knee and black cigar, nodding to us every trip. But [the] team got in and wrote on one door "Ladies" and on the other "Gents" and on [the] bath "Both Sex". We fetched house dick who clutched towel and rubbed it off blushing like fire.' In 2003 the Monteleone named a new suite after Eudora Welty. It has a fine granite bath with jacuzzi tub and a glass shower – and nothing inappropriate written on the door.

LE CHÂTEAU FRONTENAC, QUÉBEC CITY (1893)
FAIRMONT LE CHÂTEAU FRONTENAC

Château Frontenac is one of those hotels that is so well known that it's become the image of the city that it serves. More than that, its quasi-medieval turrets, monolithic great tower and steep Loire-style roofs are often used as a symbol for Canada itself.

The hotel we see today was the work of three architects over some 30 years. If the building is uniquely arresting, however, its location is remarkable too: a cliff-top overlooking a bend in the mighty, often ice-laden St Lawrence River.

Château St Louis, the first fortress built up here, was for the use of the seventeenth-century explorer and 'Father of New France' Samuel de Champlain after whom the Petit Champlain quarter on the quayside below is now named. Over the next hundred years British troops frequently burned down the residence of the French governor, eventually replacing it with Château Haldimand, named after the first governor of British Québec who was appointed in 1778.

By the late nineteenth century, Château Haldimand was too ancient to be of use and its commanding position seemed an obvious place for a new hotel. Canadian Pacific Railways had reached Québec in 1885 and in 1890 they commissioned Eugène-Étienne Taché to design a 'Fortress Hotel' in keeping with their chosen location.

Taché had already designed Québec's parliament building but in the end his plans were passed over in favour of an American architect, Bruce Price, the pioneer of US Shingle style. Canadian Pacific commissioned Price to create a different kind of building, a modern hotel whose name would be Château Frontenac after an early governor of French Québec, Louis de Buade, Comte de Frontenac et de Palluau.

Despite his modernist brief, Price drew on the work of Taché and others to design a hotel that looked like a castle of the Loire – where Comte de Frontenac had had his home – but built on a massive scale. 'The hotel is placed in the centre of a big landscape,' he wrote. 'And hence needs every advantage of bigness, both from the materials and the simplicity of its designs.'

Price's chateau was built in a horseshoe shape surrounding a huge courtyard facing away from the river. Its steep green copper roofs contrasted with red Scottish brick and local grey La Chevrotière stone quarried for the foundations and casements.

The new hotel was opened on 18 December 1893 but such was its popularity with travellers that Price was soon asked to add an extra wing along Rue Mont Carmel. This addition, opened in 1899, effectively closed off the horseshoe-shaped courtyard. It was called the Citadel Wing because it faced south towards the nineteenth-century fortress that guarded the river. Price's original design had been deliberately asymmetrical, suggesting a castle that had grown over the centuries, so further accretions fitted in well.

The interior design under Price was full of oak furniture and sixteenth-century-style panelling, deliberately harking back to old France but with wide modern hallways and modern amenities such as glass postal chutes on the landings, allowing letters from any floor to drop down into the lobby for collection.

The British novelist and dandy, Sir Max Pemberton, described the hotel a 'a great hostelry like no other one can name – majestic in the fashion of a medieval fortress, yet as up-to-date as any hotel in America and more comfortable than most.' Pemberton added with his customary extravagance:

'See Naples and then die? Rather see Québec and find a new inspiration to live.'

There were 170 rooms initially, 93 of which had private bathrooms, and all with fireplaces, making a huge demand on staff who would be tending them through the long winters.

Canadian Pacific's plan had been to appeal primarily to wealthy tourists in Canada and the United States, but the quality of their many railway hotels brought in Europeans too and Château Frontenac kept expanding. Price died in 1903 at the age of 47, so Walter S. Painter was commissioned to design the next new wing, named Mont Carmel after the opposite shore of the St Lawrence. This opened in 1910 but then in 1915 a turret to link the Citadel and Carmel Wings was added, and then finally in 1924 came the massive finishing touch. Montreal architect Edward Maxwell, who had spent the last fifteen years designing stations for Canadian Pacific Railways, was called in with his brother William. They were told to double the hotel's current capacity by adding 658 new rooms and sixteen suites.

Rather than extending further into the city, the brothers designed a gargantuan tower that would fill in the courtyard and gather all the wings to it, thereby linking them. It would have bedrooms on seventeen floors and a steeply pitched roof to dwarf all the roofs below. The undertaking was daring and made all the more impressive because its foundations could not be blasted out since the existing hotel surrounded the building site. Slowly a great crater was excavated to support the massive tower.

Edward Maxwell died during the building process, leaving William to work, like Price, on both the exterior and interior design. Through the Director-General of Historical Monuments in Paris, Maxwell was able to get historic items of French furniture copied in bulk for the Frontenac.

Photo: Bernard Gagnon

By the early 1920s the building as we recognise it today from the St Lawrence River was nearing completion. However, in January 1926 Price's original Riverview Wing caught fire. The water used to douse the flames froze on the ruins, creating a tangled and fantastic ice palace overlooking Petit Champlain. The directors immediately ordered for it to be rebuilt exactly as it had been before. Posters pinned up across North America and Europe had fixed the design in the public imagination and that design was proving lucrative.

GUEST BOOK

Inevitably such a magnificent building has had far more than its fair share of dignitaries and celebrities. During the Second World War Winston Churchill, Franklin D. Roosevelt, and Canadian prime minister Mackenzie King chose it for two strategy conferences.

Just about every visiting royal person has stayed at the Frontenac. Queen Elizabeth II's first visit was in 1951 as Duchess of Edinburgh. World leaders have included Charles de Gaulle, Princess Grace of Monaco, Chiang Kai-shek, Ronald Reagan, and François Mitterrand. In 1953 Alfred Hitchcock based his film *I Confess* (with Montgomery Clift and Anne Baxter) at the hotel. The list of stars from America, Britain and France who have taken rooms at the Frontenac is as impressive as it is predictable, but anyone who stays at Château Frontenac is always going to eclipsed by the building itself. No roster of famous names can tell its story better than its appearance. It is a star among hotels.

In the 1990s a new extension was added at the back of the Mont Carmel Wing, but subtly and in the hotel's own style. Having become a national symbol, all changes at the hotel now have to be invisible. As hotel bedrooms grew bigger in the twentieth century, the hotel's capacity shrank to a mere 611 rooms but the management continue to prove themselves resourceful in finding attic spaces left in those great roofs to create more bedrooms when they can.

Today Château Frontenac is said to be the most photo-graphed hotel in the world. That's certainly a believable boast.

THE ALGONQUIN, NEW YORK (1902)

Poor Albert Foster has gone down in history as a footnote even though he founded one of the most famous hotels in New York. In 1902, as the owner of the brand-new Puritan Hotel in Manhattan he hired a manager. Foster had named this skinny 174-room French Renaissance-style hotel after his Puritan Realty Company but the eager 31-year-old new manager, Frank Case, thought it a bad choice. He informed Foster the name was 'cold, forbidding and grim'. 'You think yourself so smart,' replied the owner. 'Suppose you find a better name?' As the Iroquois Hotel had recently opened further along West 44th Street, Case chose the name of a more local native tribe: the Algonquin.

Albert Foster's hotel did very well under Frank Case, who pretty much treated it as his own from the beginning, before taking over the lease in 1907 and raising the money to buy it outright in 1927. It was Frank Case's hospitality and flair for

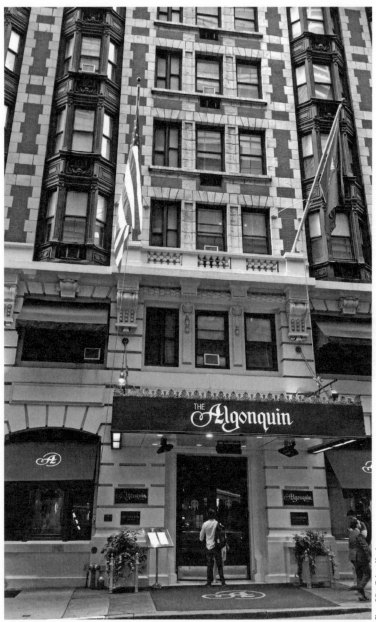

publicity that made the 'Gonk' such a popular place among the literati of Manhattan's theatreland. By 1919 the mob of voluble writers who were squeezing in together to eat in the hotel's Pergola Room had grown so large that Case moved them into the Rose Room next door. He then thoughtfully provided a large round table where they could all be seated.

So the Algonquin Round Table (also known to its members as the Vicious Circle) was formed. For over a decade journalists and authors like Alexander Woollcott, George S. Kaufman, Robert Benchley, Robert E. Sherwood, and Dorothy Parker took long lunches there, often six days a week. Harpo Marx, a friend of Woollcott's, came along too, later explaining his presence with the words: 'Somebody had to listen.'

At the age of 25, drama critic Dorothy Parker was the youngest of the group and has since become the poster girl for the Algonquin. In New York she became famous as a writer and wit, and as the prototype for other people's wise-cracking characters.

Philip Barry created a 'Dottie' clone in *Hotel Universe* (1932), as did George Oppenheimer in *Here Today* (1932), and George S. Kaufman in *Merrily We Roll Along* (1934). Kaufman's representation of Mrs Parker as the heavy-drinking, acerbic and unfashionably dressed Julia Glenn precipitated a breach between Dorothy and her former Round Table comrade. She was avenged in the end, however, outstripping him in fame, with Kaufman admitting wearily: 'Everything I've ever said will be credited to Dorothy Parker.'

Mrs Parker also lived intermittently at the Algonquin. In 1924 after she split – for the second time – from her husband, stockbroker Eddie Pond Parker, she moved into a furnished suite on the second floor. She lived there again after the

Vicious Circle began to disband in 1929 and again in 1932, when she attempted suicide in her room.

Frank Case was unperturbed as his most famous guests went their separate ways. 'What became of the reservoir at Fifth Avenue and 42nd Street?' he wrote. 'These things do not last forever. The Round Table lasted longer than any unorganised group that I know of.' In any case, a new Algonquin tradition was under way in 1930. Case had just adopted a stray cat that the actor John Barrymore christened 'Hamlet'. *Hamlet* was Barrymore's last great theatrical success before becoming a movie star.

Since then there has always been a hotel cat, to date seven toms named Hamlet and three queens named Matilda. The heavy-drinking Barrymore inspired another hotel tradition when in 1933 he convinced Frank Case to put blue gels over the lighting in what became known as the Blue Bar. Barrymore was convinced the colour improved one's appearance. Even though the Algonquin created a new cocktail bar in 2013, it is still lit by blue light.

Frank Case died in 1946 and the hotel was bought by a couple from Charleston who had previously stayed there 22 years ago on their honeymoon. Ben and Mary Bodne were impressed during that first sojourn at the Algonquin when they realised who else was in residence: the actors Tom Mix and Douglas Fairbanks Snr, the singer Eddie Cantor, and Sinclair Lewis, who would go on to be the first US writer to receive the Nobel Prize for Literature. In 1946 the Bodnes paid $1,000,000 for their new home and found the hotel a perfect fit for them. The ebullient Mary once made her chicken soup for ailing theatrical knight, Laurence Olivier. On another occasion she found herself in one of the creaky old hotel lifts with the writers William Faulkner and Thornton Wilder. 'Surely you boys know each other?' she asked. As they didn't, she introduced them.

For decade upon decade the Algonquin attracted celebrity visitors who would be welcomed by Mary from her armchair in the lobby-lounge.

MUSIC AT THE GONK

Noël Coward often stayed while performing in New York and once spilled Tallulah Bankhead's bourbon over the Algonquin's carpet. Lerner and Loewe made so much noise composing 'I Could Have Danced All Night' for *My Fair Lady* in the suite below Ben Bodne's that he threatened to throw their grand piano out of the window. Rob Reiner discovered the eighteen-year-old Harry Connick Jnr singing cabaret at the hotel and brought him in for the *When Harry Met Sally* soundtrack. The movie won Connick his first Grammy Award.

In 1987 Ben Bodne sold the hotel to investors rather than have to install new lifts. He died soon after but Mary lived on in her apartment until 2000, dying at the age of 93. She saw several different owners make refurbishments in that time and after one revamp commented: 'What I've seen looks very nice but it will never look like my old Algonquin.'

The most recent makeover was completed in 2013 at a cost of $100 million. The Round Table Room (formerly Frank Case's Oak Room) was restored to a clubland style of dark wood panelling but sadly no large round table was installed. Instead a busy and slightly demonic painting by twenty-first-century artist Natalie Ascencios presides. *Vicious Circle* depicts Harold Ross in the foreground, reading his *New*

Yorker magazine, with Alexander Woollcott leaning over his shoulder while Dorothy Parker sits, poised but brittle, to the left of the picture.

So many famous names have been associated with this remarkable hotel, including those great hoteliers Frank Case and Mary Bodne, that it seems a shame that Albert Foster, the man who built Manhattan's original Puritan Hotel, is a footnote now, remembered just for hiring Frank Case and letting him make the Algonquin his own.

PLAZA HOTEL, NEW YORK (1907)

The Plaza is a New York hotel that cannot help generating headlines.

The current building is the second hotel of that name on the south-east edge of Central Park. The first was a blunt, square eight-storey brick building constructed on the site of the headquarters of the Skating Club of New York (founded 1863).

In the 1880s the invention of refrigerated surfaces enabled the club to relocate to an indoor space and the first Plaza Hotel was built, opening in 1890. That was demolished in 1905. It was replaced by a white brick hotel that adopted the French château style then so popular in Europe, stretching it to nineteen storeys high. The new Plaza opened in October 1907. It had been designed by Henry Janeway Hardenbergh who had planned both the original Waldorf (1893) and Astoria (1897). Those hotels were later joined together to make the Waldorf-Astoria and then demolished in 1929 to make way for the Empire State Building. New York at the beginning of the twentieth century was continually demolishing itself to build higher and higher.

The men behind the new Plaza were the hotelier Fred Sterry, financier Bernhard Beinecke and Harry S. Black, president of the Fuller Construction Company who also constructed the Flatiron Building and in due course turned a suite on the eighteenth floor of the Plaza into his own private duplex.

Hardenbergh's Plaza Hotel cost $12.5 million to construct. The Dutch-American architect spared none of his clients' money. This new Plaza contained 1,650 crystal chandeliers and its order for gold-rimmed china was the largest ever placed with Straus & Sons, New York's main importer of china, porcelain and crockery (and later the owners of Macy's).

The Plaza was for a short while the tallest building in that section of town. Its ostentatious grandeur lured in the wealthy and the distinguished. The Vanderbilts maintained an extensive apartment, the British Field Marshal Kitchener came to stay and so did the newly married Scott and Zelda Fitzgerald who lived in a $200-a-week suite at the Plaza. On one occasion a drunken Scott tried to go swimming in the shallow Pulitzer Fountain outside the hotel. This was the Jazz Age after all.

In 1917 Edna Woolworth, youngest daughter of the phenomenally rich F.W., committed suicide at the Plaza, and in 1926 her older sister Jessie was robbed of $683,000 worth of jewels stolen from her suite while she was in the bath. The newspapers devoured these stories.

The hotel has also led a high-profile life in fiction. In Fitzgerald's *The Great Gatsby* (1925), his narrator Nick Carraway meets Jordan Baker in the Plaza's tea garden. There is also a confrontation between Gatsby and Tom Buchanan in a suite they've taken for an afternoon drinking party.

Other books set at the hotel have included the *Eloise* series by Kay Thompson about a young girl who lives at the Plaza, and *The Princess Diaries* by Meg Cabot, where the heroine's royal grandmother bases herself at the Plaza while in New York.

The Plaza has also featured in many films, from a dramatisation of *Eloise* in 1956 to *American Hustle* in 2013. Along the way Hitchcock used it as a location in *North by Northwest* with Cary Grant (1959), as did William Wyler in *Funny Girl* (1968), Nora Ephron in *Sleepless in Seattle* (1993), and Woody Allen in *Hollywood Ending* (2002).

Real-life high-profile guests have included the photographer Cecil Beaton, who famously photographed Greta Garbo smoking in his suite (Rooms 249–251) in 1946. In 1956, the year she married Arthur Miller, Marilyn Monroe caused a sensation at a Plaza press conference when the strap on her dress broke. The Beatles also gave a press conference in 1964 while staying at the Plaza. It was described euphemistically as 'lively'.

Another celebrated name who made headlines at the hotel was Truman Capote. By June 1966 he had decided his 'non-fiction novel' *In Cold Blood* had made enough money for him to celebrate it (and himself) with the lavish and legendary Black and White Ball.

The hotel has also been famous for musicians who have performed in its function rooms, including the ubiquitous Josephine Baker and Marlene Dietrich as well as Liza Minnelli. In 1958 Miles Davis recorded a live session in the Persian Room which was finally released on vinyl in 1974.

Two political daughters also made headlines at the Plaza. In 1967 the 41-year-old Svetlana Alliluyeva, only daughter of Josef Stalin, defected to the United States and gave her first press conference at the Plaza. Two years later, Julie Nixon, daughter of the incumbent President, was married to former President Eisenhower's grandson at the hotel.

There has also been plenty of drama centred on the various owners of the hotel. The Plaza was bought in 1943 by the visionary but eccentric hotelier Conrad Hilton, who was later given a cameo appearance in the 1956 TV show of *Eloise*. (Ironically, this dramatisation of Kay Thompson's books was filmed in California not New York.) Donald J. Trump bought the hotel in 1988. When the 1992 movie *Home Alone 2*, partly shot in the Plaza, was made, he insisted on a cameo appearance in it.

SILENT ROOMS

Since a major refurbishment in 2006 the Plaza has reduced to 282 rooms while more than half of its accommodation – the elevation facing Central Park – is now given over to private apartments. Sadly this means that the original marble lobby with its four ornate elevators is no longer open to the public. Neither is the famous Oak Room dining room, nor the Oak Bar. Both stand empty but in perfect condition awaiting reanimation one day.

The side entrance on Grand Army Plaza, originally intended for those alighting from carriages, now admits hotel guests into a side lobby hung with a massive Russian chandelier, one of four purchased by Donald Trump's wife Marla.

Trump installed his first wife Ivana as the hotel's president. Five years later in 1993 he married his second wife, Marla Maples, in the Plaza's ballroom. The maverick property tycoon spent $50 million on hotel renovations but in a prepackaged bankruptcy deal in 1992 he ceded a 49 per cent stake to a group of US banks in exchange for forgiveness of $250 million in debts.

In March 2014 the current owner, Subatra Roy, the second largest employer in India, was arrested for failing to appear in court over non-payment of debts. He attempted to sell his majority stake in the Plaza for $4 billion but did not find a buyer.

Meanwhile Donald Trump went on to become the most controversial American president in history. The Plaza just can't help making news.

COPACABANA PALACE, RIO DE JANEIRO (1923)
BELMOND COPACABANA PALACE

In 1917 the Mayor of Rio de Janeiro issued a decree decriminalising sea-bathing at Leme and Copacabana. The hours for this European indulgence would be from 5.00–8.00am and from 5.00–7.00pm. It was from this unpromising start that the famous Copacabana Palace arose.

In 1892 a tunnel from the capital to the almost inaccessible beaches had been created but a lot of coastal tenements had to be cleared before promenades like Avenida Atlântica could be created. Brazil's centenary celebrations were due in 1922 and President Pessoa was determined to dazzle Europeans with the beauty of Copacabana Beach.

A grand new international hotel was planned to lodge guests. It would be the best hotel in South America. In the event only delegations from Portugal and Argentina turned up, but by then the hotel was under way.

To manage this project Pessoa brought in Octávio Guinle, the black sheep of a family who owned the best hotels in Rio and São Paulo. Guinle agreed to take charge as long as the new Copacabana Palace operated its own casino to make it financially viable. Pessoa initially agreed, but his successor reneged in 1924, banning gambling throughout Brazil.

By this time Guinle had bought an entire city block on the Avenida. He had also commissioned a French architect, Joseph Gire, who came up with a Neoclassical façade reminiscent of the Carlton in Cannes and the Negresco Hotel in Nice. Its ground floor was given over to restaurants, ballrooms and a theatre where the casino would have stood.

Guinle and Gire were very ambitious. Like so many of their contemporaries they imported only the best: not just chandeliers from Czechoslovakia and carpets from England, but even cement from Germany.

Despite an attempted coup taking place along Avenida Atlântica at one point during the hotel's construction, it opened in August 1923 with a grand gala. 'Today the most grandiose and luxurious example of South American architecture will be launched by Rio high society', the local press were told to report.

Like a true obsessive – and hotel ownership does encourage extreme behaviour – Guinle installed himself in one of the two presidential suites and ruled his new hotel with a rod of iron. Punctuality was insisted upon for staff and for guests. Gentlemen were not permitted to dine or attend a performance in the hotel's theatre without a jacket and tie, regardless of the heat.

From the beginning, Guinle's hotel marketed itself brilliantly and relentlessly. International celebrity names were invited to visit. One of the first was Albert Einstein, who lectured on his theory of relativity and was given lunch at the hotel. In 1927 Julio de Caro was commissioned to compose the 'Copacabana Tango'. Its sheet music sold all round the world and spread the name Copacabana to households that possessed a piano but would never travel to Brazil. In New York the famous Copacabana Club opened on East 60th Street, just one more example of how the hotel was making itself a byword for glamour.

In 1923 the playboy sons of George V of England, Prince Edward and Prince George, came to stay at the Copacabana Palace, dining there and bathing in the sea in front of the hotel. Unsubstantiated accounts exist of the royal pair getting seriously inebriated too. When the *Graf Zeppelin* dirigible made its maiden flight into the southern hemisphere in 1930, Guinle ensured its route into Rio was directly over the Copacabana Palace and that photos were taken to prove this.

The Second World War hardly touched the nightly festivities in Rio's most glamorous hotel, although blackout on the beach did lead to opportunistic couples being arrested for indecency.

After the war Octávio Guinle continued to steer the hotel through difficult times. In 1946 he saw the casino he had been promised in 1923 – and joyfully opened under a subsequent president – closed down for good by the new president, Marshal Dutra.

By the 1950s the hotel was once again established as an international institution, hosting jet-set celebrities and Rat Pack entertainers. It was also a focal point for Rio society, its half Olympic-length swimming pool becoming the headquarters of the Clube dos Cafajestes (the Scoundrels' Club). These young men were the sons of the wealthiest families in Rio – including Octávio's son Jorginho – and their wild behaviour was curbed by only one rule: 'Respect the wife of your friend.' Unfortunately everyone else's wives were fair game and a lot of fights ensued. In 1953 while Octávio Guinle was in Europe, Jorginho let his Cafajestes into the Presidential Suite to celebrate the divorce of one of their number, a Dominican playboy called Porfirio Rubirosa, from Woolworth heiress Barbara Hutton.

Fortunately back in 1946 Octávio Guinle had hired Oscar Ornstein, a German public relations manager, to keep the hotel's name in the press. Now Ornstein became adept at keeping the hotel's name out of the newspapers. This led to the Copacabana Palace becoming a discreet place for wealthy people who needed privacy. The hotel's new annex, opened in 1947, was soon rumoured to be a hotbed of illicit celebrity romance. One star who was definitely protected by the hotel was Brazilian singer and entertainer Carmen Miranda, who in 1954 holed up in the Palace for four months suffering severe depression after the collapse of her Hollywood marriage.

Then in 1960 the capital of Brazil moved to Brasilia and Rio began a decline that also affected the Copacabana Palace. The death of Octávio Guinle in 1968 and the discovery of massive debts caused by his impossibly high standards hastened this process.

The hotel limped on but in 1989 it was sold to James Sherwood who had set up Orient Express. Sherwood had often stayed at the hotel and was a fan of Joseph Gire's architecture. And so funds were found to begin the hotel's revival. Despite some proposals by spirited architects to demolish and rebuild anew, Sherwood's company (since 2014 renamed as Belmond) has kept to the promise made by Philip Carruthers, the new managing director whom Sherwood installed. 'The future of the Copacabana Palace is not open to debate. It was defined in 1923 when Octávio

Guinle opened the doors of the monument he had brought into existence.'

ORSON WELLES

In 1942 Orson Welles arrived at the Copacabana Palace, supposedly to make a propaganda film for the war effort, but partly running away from completion difficulties with two Hollywood films he was directing, *The Magnificent Ambersons* and *Journey into Fear.* Welles stayed eight months at the hotel, during which time he drank and ate heavily, laboriously heaving his bulk out of the swimming pool and frequenting Rio's brothels. On one occasion, after an argument with his girlfriend Dolores Del Rio, he threw furniture from his hotel suite into the swimming pool.

After using up most of his propaganda-film budget, Welles suddenly switched – without permission from his studio – to retelling on film the true story of four heroic Brazilian fishermen. Unfortunately one of them was drowned by the swell from a production launch. At this point the studio broke all connection with Welles, who had to sell some of his US assets to pay the massive bill he'd run up at the Palace.

ROYAL HAWAIIAN, WAIKIKI (1927)

Waikiki Beach, three miles south-east of Honolulu, was a retreat for Hawaiian royalty during the 1800s. Kings and their families surfed here on early versions of the longboard. By the 1880s, in response to the increasing number of foreign visitors, King Kalākaua allowed a few small hotels to open along the beach, including one called Sans Souci where Robert Louis Stevenson stayed in September and October 1893 before returning to Samoa (where he died the following year).

At this time there already was a Royal Hawaiian Hotel located in Honolulu itself. It was a splendid wooden structure with broad verandas built at the command of the energetic King Kamehameha V in 1872. It was the king himself who insisted it was given the regal appellation, but as more and more hotels were built on the shore to answer tourist appetite for palm-fronded beaches, the inland Royal Hawaiian went into decline and was eventually demolished.

Following the deposition of the monarchy and the annexation of Hawaii as an American territory in 1893, tourism from America's west coast looked set to expand. In 1901 a tall, white wood-framed structure known as the Moana was built on Waikiki Beach. This was Hawaii's first beach hotel that wasn't just a collection of picturesque huts. Despite the bankruptcy of two of its owners, the Moana continued to fill its 75 guest rooms. It dominated Hawaiian tourism until 1927 when a new Royal Hawaiian was opened between the old Moana Hotel and the bungalow complex known as the Halekulani.

The men behind this new venture were Captain William Matson, owner of the Matson Steamship Company, and his son-in-law, a former stockbroker called William P. Roth. Roth had convinced Captain Matson that there was money to be made from bringing cruise ships from the US to Hawaii but only if there were a great hotel waiting at the end of the journey. In the 1920s it took four days for west-coast

Americans to reach Hawaii – as long as it did for east-coast Americans to reach Europe. And the hotels in Europe were much classier than the current Moana and Halekulani.

Matson and Roth found investors to create the Territorial Hotel Company and purchased a fifteen-acre parcel of beach front for hotel development. The move was unpopular locally as this meant building on Helumoa, the personal playground of the deposed monarchy. In the nineteenth century Queen Kaahumanu (1768–1832), the favourite wife of the mighty first King Kamehameha, had built her summer palace in a coconut grove on this very site.

The Territorial Hotel Company pressed ahead but more problems followed as the American architects of the new Royal Hawaiian, Warren and Wetmore, had neglected to visit the site before designing their ambitious structure of stucco-faced sandstone. Unaware that the south wing of this extremely heavy hotel would be built over a swamp, Warren and Wetmore soon found its walls were disappearing into quicksand. A retired naval engineer was brought in who inserted girders and large concrete blocks into the foundations to stabilise the hotel (they can still be seen in the basement). By this stage the budget for the largest building in the Pacific at that time had risen to a massive $4 million.

When completed, the hotel, an H shape with spurs running off in all directions, finally cost over $5 million. It was topped off with Moorish-style towers and painted shocking pink. This pseudo-Spanish style had no reference point in Hawaiian culture, but was fashionable in the States because of the 'Latin lover' films of Rudolf Valentino that were a big box office draw on the mainland.

The new Royal had a 'Regency' ballroom decorated with murals of barges floating down the River Nile, and eight Chinese lobby boys in coolie jackets who were in charge of

Photo: Daniel Ramirez

luggage. The outdoor dining space was called the Persian Room and decorated in a Middle Eastern style. There were 400 en-suite bedrooms with rugs imported from Czechoslovakia, Tunisia, Holland and Iran. There were bamboo awnings over all windows. It would be fair to say that the hotel was designed to emanate an all-purpose exoticism.

The newly appointed manager, an Italian called Arthur Bengalia, was given a budget that allowed him to compete with the best European hotels. A staff of 300 included 40 room boys, twenty bellboys, ten elevator operators, two doormen and two pages. Three men were employed full-time just to keep the 800 palm trees trimmed. Bengalia was understandably terrified that the reputation of his tropical paradise could be ruined at any time by a rogue coconut falling on a guest's head.

The hotel opened on 1 February 1927 with a black-tie gala attended by over 1,200 guests, including the US Territorial Governor Wallace R. Farrington, and Princess Abigail Campbell Kawānanakoa, heir to the Hawaiian throne. Princess Kawānanakoa signed in as the hotel's first guest but did not stay. A pageant that she directed that evening celebrated the achievements of the first King Kamehameha who had unified these islands in the eighteenth century, but it was dismissed as 'colourful and semi-barbaric' by the local press. In 1927 the Royal Hawaiian was not aimed at people wishing to explore indigenous culture.

Two years later the Great Depression struck, bankrupting the Territorial Hotel Company, but the Matson and Roth's Matson Line bought out the other partners. The Royal Hawaiian recovered its prosperity during the 1930s and a visit from Franklin D. Roosevelt, greeted with a traditional *lei*, in July 1934 sealed the hotel's pre-eminent status on Hawaii.

After the attack at Pearl Harbor the Royal Hawaiian was

requisitioned for use by the US Navy as an R&R facility. The only concessions to the war were a lot of barbed wire on the beach – in case the Japanese came back – and the locking up of all the wines and spirits behind a camouflaged door in the hotel cellar. The Coconut Bar was turned into a soda fountain for the duration. Sobriety was supposed to reign, but the mariners found many ways around that, as mariners always do.

On 1 February 1947, twenty years to the day after the gala opening in 1927, the Royal Hawaiian – now universally known as the Pink Palace – reopened following a complete post-war restoration.

These days what was once the tallest building in Waikiki is dwarfed by the high-rise hotels around it, but the Palace sits at the centre of it all with the kind of calm dignity that comes with great age.

LIFE AT THE ROYAL HAWAIIAN

The presentation of Hawaiian *leis* is a tradition that has survived from the hotel's earliest days, but much else about the guest experience has changed. Before the Second World War guests would usually arrive on the Matson Line's SS *Malolo* and be greeted at the quayside by the Royal Hawaiian Orchestra. Many visitors brought their own cars in the hold of the *Malolo* and most brought servants. The first couple to check in on 1 February 1927 were Major and Mrs Douglas King of London who arrived with their maid and valet, and took four rooms. After such a long journey the average stay was measured in weeks rather than days.

BILTMORE HOTEL, MIAMI (1931)
MIAMI-BILTMORE HOTEL AND COUNTRY CLUB

Miami's Biltmore Hotel has had a dramatic life encompassing royalty and mobsters, hurricanes and zombies. It was designed in the 1920s by the New York architects, Schultze and Weaver, whose speciality was skyscraper hotels like the Atlanta Biltmore Hotel, the Breakers in Palm Beach, and the new Waldorf-Astoria in New York (which, on its completion in 1931, was the world's tallest hotel until 1963, when it was surpassed by Moscow's Hotel Ukraina).

The client was George Merrick, creator of the Coral Gables development, a residential resort-city of affluent tree-lined boulevards, golf courses and country clubs. At its centre Merrick wanted a statement hotel, and so in 1925 he brought in John McEntee Bowman, founder of the already famous Biltmore hotel chain. The budget was $10 million and it showed. When the hotel opened its great arms towards Anastasia Avenue in March 1926 it was, at 315 feet, the tallest building in Florida. Two years later Dade County Courthouse would eclipse the Biltmore in height. (Despite an abundance of land this was the golden age of competitive skyscrapers in America.) The new Biltmore made a dramatic impact with a central tower, illuminated at night, that was modelled on the bell tower of Seville cathedral. It also had for decades the largest swimming pool in the world.

Coral Gables itself was part of the Florida land boom, a Jazz Age phenomenon that transformed the east coast of this hot and swampy state. Twentieth-century innovations like effective insecticides, air conditioning and refrigeration made a big difference, but so did unprecedented affluence. Big bands headed south to entertain the phenomenally wealthy. Gangsters followed suit, including Al Capone who was said to have plotted Chicago's Valentine's Day massacre while in Miami.

WHAT'S IN A NAME?

In 1888, as a young and extremely wealthy young man of 25, George Vanderbilt visited Asheville in North Carolina. In the Blue Ridge Mountains he found what he considered the perfect location for a country home, which he built in the fashionable French chateau style. It took six years to create what became known as America's premier home. Vanderbilt gave it the name Biltmore because his ancestors were from Bildt in Holland and the house was built on open rolling moorland.

It was not uncommon in the nineteenth century for distinguished names like Waldorf, Astor, Connaught, or Grosvenor to be used for hotels without family connection or even permission. The name Biltmore was appropriated by a number of US enterprises, so to differentiate his hotel chain from any other Biltmores, the Canadian hotelier John Bowman created the Bowman-Biltmore Hotels Corporation.

In the 1920s the Corporation opened Biltmore hotels in California, Arizona, Florida, Ohio, Rhode Island, Georgia, and New York.

John Bowman also took on the management of other hotels. Many of Bowman's hotels had multi-storey garages attached, which is why in *Guys and Dolls* the gamblers who are trying to find somewhere for an all-important crap game sing: 'The Biltmore garage wants a grand, But we ain't got a grand on hand.'

Photo: Luis Villa

In the months following the Biltmore's opening it seemed there was more money in Miami than anyone could spend, but the guests did their best. Then within six months, disaster struck. On 18 September the Miami Hurricane, the costliest storm ever in terms of damage (sums adjusted to present-day levels), hit the United States. Over 500 people were killed and 43,000 were left homeless. The hotel, three miles inland, was hardly damaged – in fact it provided shelter for over 2,000 displaced persons – but the disaster signalled the end of the land boom and conspicuous consumption. Florida was not a state to be trusted.

The Biltmore recovered, but it also gained a certain notoriety when in March 1929 the narcotics gangster Thomas 'Fatty' Walsh, associate of Dutch Schultz and 'Lucky' Luciano, was killed on the hotel's thirteenth floor during an argument about gambling debts. It's claimed that his ghost still haunts the hotel elevator, opening and closing the doors unpredictably at that floor.

In October that same year the Wall Street Crash made life difficult for anyone whose investments were overstretched – as is almost always the case with real estate developers. George Merrick's Coral Gables development declared bankruptcy. In December 1929 Bowman bought out his partner for a mere $2,100,000. Two years later Bowman resold the hotel at a profit to millionaire Henry Latham Doherty and with his generous backing the Biltmore survived the early 1930s.

This was the Biltmore's true heyday. It played host to 1930s 'royalty', not just the itinerant Duke and Duchess of Windsor, but Ginger Rogers, Judy Garland, Bing Crosby and various members of the Roosevelt family. FDR had a temporary White House office set up at the hotel for when he vacationed on fishing trips in Miami. Even the Vanderbilts of that first Biltmore in North Carolina were frequent guests.

It's been estimated that in those days as many as 3,000

locals would come out on Sunday afternoons to watch the synchronised swimmers, the bathing beauties and alligator wrestling in the pool. Johnny Weissmuller, before making his Tarzan debut in 1932, broke one of his many swimming world records at the Biltmore's Olympic-sized pool. Often guests would stay on after the poolside entertainment to go tea dancing on the hotel's terrace.

This golden era came to an end in November 1942 when the War Department took over the Biltmore and converted it to a 1,200-bed hospital. Many of the windows were sealed with concrete, and the marble floors covered with linoleum. Sadly in 1946, rather than resuming its career as a hotel, the Biltmore was transferred from the Army to the Veterans Health Administration, eventually becoming part of the University of Miami's School of Medicine. It closed completely in 1968 and was boarded up.

In 1973, through the Historic Monuments Act, the City of Coral Gables was granted ownership of the Biltmore but it remained empty. In 1977 its extravagant but decaying interiors were used as the setting for Ken Wiederhorn's 1977 cult horror film *Shock Waves* in which Peter Cushing played a former SS commander battling with a force of subterranean Nazi zombies in a deserted hotel.

Finally in 1983, the city embarked on a full restoration. It took four years and $55 million to reopen the hotel on 31 December 1987 as a luxury resort hotel with – some might think inappropriately – its own Al Capone Suite.

When the hotel originally opened in 1926 Dr Frank Crane, influential author of *Everyday Wisdom,* predicted: 'Many people will come and go, but this structure will remain a thing of lasting beauty.' He was proved right when 70 years later in 1996 it became one of only 21 US hotels designated National Historic Landmarks.

UNITED KINGDOM

THE LANGHAM, LONDON (1865)

In no other city in the world are so many historic hotels still in business as they are in London. Brown's (1837) and Fleming's (1851) were both carved out of old Mayfair town houses and are still in operation. Claridge's, opened in 1854 but completely rebuilt in 1898, is also still in business. Two of London's earliest railway hotels, the Great Northern at King's Cross (1854) and the Grosvenor in Victoria (1862), have recently been extensively renovated and reopened. But the city's first *purpose-built* grand hotel is the Langham, which has dominated the area south of Regent's Park since its completion in 1865.

The Langham, by its very height, by its technical innovations and the fact that it was opened by the playboy Prince of Wales (and future Edward VII), was a new development in London: a 'grand hotel' in the manner of Le Grand Hôtel Paris, which had been opened by Empress Eugénie just three years earlier. It's surprising therefore how often its survival hung in the balance.

The Langham was designed by the London architect John Giles and was his most prominent project. It took two years to build at a cost of £300,000 and when it opened in 1865 it offered 100 water closets, 36 bathrooms and the first hydraulic lifts in England (an innovation copied from Paris).

Two years after its opening, the developers, led by the

Earl of Shrewsbury, had to declare bankruptcy. No hotel in England had ever cost this much and the next owners were able to buy it for £150,000, half the construction costs.

The poor general manager, Charles Schumann, was blamed for the debacle and retired in disgrace. His replacement was a former Union Army officer named James Sanderson who helped develop the hotel's American market. In the decades following the Civil War, faster trans-Atlantic crossings were making Europe an attractive proposition for wealthy Americans.

In November 1872 the 37-year-old Mark Twain was in residence at the Langham when he published a letter in the *London Daily News* announcing that he was called home and was cancelling any further lectures in Great Britain. Another early American guest was the writer and actor Howard Paul who in 1890 described the hotel's ambitious glass-roofed Palm Court as 'a spacious courtyard decorated with palms, cypresses and picturesque, feathery green plants, as though a bit of Kew Gardens had strayed into town to enliven the metropolitan bricks and mortar.'

Hotels in London were still not yet places where ladies socialised. This was something that the Savoy would shortly pioneer. But the Langham quickly established itself as a place for gentlemen to meet for business and conviviality. In 1889 the publisher Joseph Marshall Stoddart, editor of *Lippincott's Monthly Magazine* of Philadelphia, brought two promising English writers in their thirties together for dinner at the Langham. They were Oscar Wilde and Arthur Conan Doyle. This singularly successful meal resulted in Wilde being commissioned to write *The Picture of Dorian Gray* and Conan Doyle *The Sign of the Four*, his second Sherlock Holmes novella. Arthur Conan Doyle greatly enjoyed what he called a 'golden evening' at the Langham and actually

Photo: © Kate Tadman-Mourby

used the hotel as a location in both *The Sign of the Four* and in his third Holmes story, *A Scandal in Bohemia.*

DVOŘÁK AT THE LANGHAM

In 1884 the Czech composer Antonín Dvořák was in Britain as a guest of London's Royal Philharmonic Society to conduct a series of concerts of his music. Speaking very little English and unable to discover how to get breakfast in such a huge building, Dvořák went out on foot early one morning looking for a café. He found one eventually – or so he thought – in Pall Mall, walked in and sat down. The diminutive composer soon grew annoyed that no one would serve him. Eventually it was explained to him that he was in the Athenaeum Club and could not be served unless he became a member, a process that took many, many years, assuming one was a gentleman.

The Langham, with its sumptuous Italian mosaic floors and its walls lined with 15,000 yards of Persian silk, was always an expensive enterprise to maintain. During the Great Depression of the 1930s the owners urged their property on the BBC – whose premises at Broadcasting House on the other side of Portland Place were never big enough – but the Corporation resisted.

During the London Blitz the celebrated American journalist Ed Murrow stayed at the Langham and broadcast live from its roof during Luftwaffe raids. He adopted his famous catchphrase 'Goodnight and good luck' from the black humour of the hotel porters who in 1940 never knew if they'd make it through the night.

The Blitz didn't destroy the solidly constructed hotel, but the first time it was hit in September 1940 the room of novelist J.B. Priestley was ripped to shreds. Fortunately the great man had been hauled – somewhat grumpily – out of bed to broadcast to Canada that night. In December 1940 four floors of the western wing were destroyed but the hotel soldiered on until its water tanks were fractured; 38,000 gallons flooded through the Langham and it had to be closed.

In the 1950s the patched-up building was occupied by the BBC as ancillary office space, and in 1965 the corporation purchased it outright with a view to eventual redevelopment. The handsome Palm Court became the radio reference library and the restaurant where Wilde and Doyle had dined became the BBC Club. With its floors and walls boarded over, the Langham no longer looked like a hotel at all.

In 1980 the BBC applied to demolish the building and replace it with a modern office development designed by Norman Foster that would have been wholly out of keeping with the style of Portland Place. (The cluster of buildings around the Langham has created an unexpectedly harmonious mix of John Nash Regency, Langham Victoriana and Broadcasting House Art Deco.) Unable to get planning permission, the BBC finally sold the property – at a huge profit – to the Ladbroke Group who reopened it as the Langham Hilton Hotel in 1991 after a £100 million refurbishment. The initial redesign was florid in a very 1990s way, with a dramatic Russian vodka bar (the hotel featured in the 1995 James Bond film *GoldenEye*, doubling for St Petersburg's Grand Hotel Europe).

In 2009 the Langham went through another costly reinvention when it became the flagship of Dr Lo Ka Shui's

Langham Hotels and Resorts. No longer under threat of demolition or redevelopment, the Langham suddenly found itself a much-prized icon and brand name with ten 'daughter' hotels around the world, from Boston to Sydney, Shanghai to Jakarta.

The Langham has confounded the expectations of the twentieth century to prove itself a great survivor, which is gratifying. After all, it was here, in this small, awkward corner site between Regent's Park and Regent Street that the story of British grand hotels began.

THE RANDOLPH, OXFORD (1866)
THE MACDONALD RANDOLPH HOTEL

In 2015 Oxford's Randolph Hotel closed for the first time in its 150-year history. A fire that began in the kitchens as a beef stroganoff was being prepared resulted in flames leaping up through the hotel's mansard roofing.

Every available fire engine tackled the blaze. Town and Gown were equally saddened. The Randolph, such a controversial structure when first opened, had become a part of Oxford life. Fortunately the damage was contained. The hotel managed to reopen within days and to refurbish completely within eleven months.

The Randolph's initial unpopularity stemmed from its being designed at a crucial and controversial time when the Gothic Revival was taking root in Britain. In 1864 everyone agreed that Oxford needed a superior commercial hotel, especially because the newly married Prince and Princess of Wales (the future Edward VII and Queen Alexandra) were scheduled to visit in two years' time. The city lacked appropriate accommodation for a royal entourage.

Plans were drawn up by local architect William Wilkinson, a cantankerous but talented man. While the Neo-Gothic design received support from men like art critic John Ruskin who were keen to promote a Protestant form of medievalism in Britain, it was condemned by many who saw Wilkinson's design as spoiling the Neoclassical lines of Beaumont Street, 'the finest ensemble of gentlemen's houses in the city'.

The proposed structure was considered too big, towering over its surroundings, and its style was in complete contrast to the rest of the street. Some went as far as to say that the Randolph was a direct insult to the building that stood opposite it: the new Ashmolean Museum, perhaps the most perfect Neoclassical building in Oxford, completed in 1845.

Nevertheless, business considerations won out in the end, as they usually do – even in Oxford – and a toned-down Neo-Gothic Randolph (minus its central spire) was built and duly opened for business in 1866.

The Randolph quickly became the place for both visiting dignitaries and visiting parents to stay when in Oxford. Years later John Betjeman, an Oxford student (1925–8) and future Poet Laureate, summed up the contrasting sides of Beaumont Street well: 'This tall, vertical Victorian hotel was a Gothic answer to the Classic vertical composition of the Ashmolean and Taylorian buildings on the other side of the road. Both buildings, despite their difference in style, were satisfactory upright terminations to the long, low Georgian curve of Beaumont Street.'

In 1894 the hotel proudly added an 'American elevator', in 1899 a ballroom, and finally in 1923 an extension down Beaumont Street, which Oxford purists had hoped would be Georgian in style this time, but the Randolph Hotel Company

once again got its Neo-Gothic way. Guests also enjoyed a billiard room, a ladies' coffee room (very much a twentieth-century innovation) and 'a conservatory for smoking'.

The guest to leave the most obvious mark on the hotel was cartoonist, art critic and stage designer Sir Osbert Lancaster whose twelve illustrations to the novel *Zuleika Dobson, an Oxford Romance* now hang in the drawing room. They were originally hung in the ballroom in 1937. According to hotel legend, the wealthy Sir Osbert paid for his stay at the Randolph with these witty depictions of Oxford student life in the years before the First World War, but that's unlikely. Lancaster was not short of money and in any case most people now assume these lively oil paintings were worked up by someone else from his drawings. (Artists who have paid for their accommodation with works of art are a common myth in hotels around the world, along with the ghost of a grey lady and the legend that Ernest Hemingway regularly propped up the hotel bar.)

In 1915, following the outbreak of the First World War, the Randolph was one of many hotels across Britain that gave up its ballroom and drawing room for convalescent soldiers returning from fighting in France and Belgium. That inconvenience aside, very few dramas dogged the hotel during the twentieth century.

For many people around the world, the Randolph these days is most closely associated with two fictional characters, Inspector Morse and Sergeant Lewis, who feature in the novels of Oxford author Colin Dexter, and their dramatisations. In both the books and the TV series Morse and Lewis regularly discuss their cases in the Randolph Bar where Morse claims, 'They serve a decent pint'. In several stories crime suspects either dine or stay at the Randolph, and in the novel *The Jewel that was Ours* (dramatised as 'The Wolvercote Tongue')

Morse investigates the suspicious death of an American hotel guest in her room.

In 2001 the bar where Colin Dexter had often sat as an extra in the TV series was officially renamed the Morse Bar. This is a hotel which makes a point of honouring its traditions, the latest of which is to refuse to serve beef stroganoff. It has been off the menu since that near-disastrous fire.

LITERARY MOMENTS AT THE RANDOLPH

Evelyn Waugh, who used the hotel as a location in *Brideshead Revisited*, once shocked diners at the Randolph by intervening loudly in a discussion of bisexuality, declaring, 'Buggers have babies'.

Kingsley Amis's future wife Hilly earned his admiration by sneaking into the hotel to wash her hair and underwear while staying with him – illicitly – across the road at St John's College.

The poet Philip Larkin and the novelist Barbara Pym, who carried out a fourteen-year epistolary relationship, finally met for lunch at the Randolph in 1975.

THE SAVOY HOTEL, LONDON (1889)

The stories of many great hotels are also family stories. The Savoy Hotel would not have existed without Richard D'Oyly Carte, nor achieved its success without Carte's second wife Helen, his son Rupert, nor indeed Rupert's daughter (and somewhat reluctant successor) Bridget D'Oyly Carte.

Carte, like so many Victorian hoteliers, was not born into the same class of the clientele that he ambitiously set out to woo. His father had been a musician and music publisher. To be honest, Richard Carte (D'Oyly was a second given name, not part of a double-barrelled surname) didn't even set out to be a hotelier. Abandoning hopes of becoming a composer, Carte priggishly promoted respectable musical entertainment in London's West End, believing it would see off the more risqué French operetta popular at the time.

He succeeded by coaxing his contemporaries, W.S. Gilbert and Sir Arthur Sullivan, back together (their first collaboration in 1871 had not been a triumph). *Trial by Jury,* a runaway success in 1875, was followed in quick succession by *HMS Pinafore* and *The Pirates of Penzance.* Carte was soon making a lot of money, but he certainly earned it. Keeping together the volatile partnership of Gilbert and Sullivan took rare diplomatic skills. Carte then formed and ran the D'Oyly Carte Opera Company to perform their works (reinforcing the idea that he had a double-barrelled surname).

In 1881, using the profits from the Gilbert and Sullivan operettas, Carte constructed a theatre where henceforth all their work would be premiered. The Savoy was built on the site of the ancient Savoy Palace in London, the latest incarnation of which had burned down in 1864. On an area of land between the theatre and the Thames embankment, Carte also built an electric generator. The Savoy Theatre was the first building in the world to be wholly lit by electricity, but Richard D'Oyly Carte had a new project in mind. This prime Thameside site was to become a luxury hotel. Having seen the opulence of American hotels during his many business trips to the United States, Carte decided to build the first US-style hotel in Britain. The Savoy was intended not just to attract the many wealthy foreigners visiting London, but the British aristocracy too.

The hotel opened on 6 August 1889. The architect was Thomas Edward Collcutt, who also designed the Palace Theatre that Carte built for his short-lived English Grand Opera Company. Collcutt was keen on red brick with pale terracotta ornamentation but Carte wanted glazed brickwork, an American innovation that would prevent London's smoke-laden air from blackening the hotel's exterior.

The hotel, like the theatre whose view of the Thames it now stole, boasted electric lights throughout and an electric elevator or 'ascending room' as it was called. This contained a sofa and took minutes to pass between floors, but it was an improvement on the old, noisy, steam-powered lifts. Other startling firsts included private en suite bathrooms in marble for most of the 268 bedrooms and hot water from the faucets that was available round the clock.

In 1890, Carte's great coup was to lure César Ritz from Hôtel de Provence in Cannes to manage the Savoy, with Auguste Escoffier as chef de cuisine. The two men were not only very good at their respective jobs, but were beloved of the aristocracy, plutocracy and royalty that Carte courted. The hotel quickly became Carte's most successful venture, more successful even than the Savoyard Operas (as Gilbert and Sullivan's works became known in 1890).

The future Edward VII – a great fan of Ritz and Escoffier – was often seen at the Savoy's Beaufort Room during the Naughty Nineties. (One night Escoffier served him frogs' legs, to the prince's great amusement.) Aristocratic English ladies who hitherto would never have dined in public were emboldened to do so by the patronage of Ritz's great champion Lady de Grey. The first British woman to smoke in public, the Duchesse de Clermont-Tonnerre, did so ostentatiously at the Savoy in 1896.

Courtesy of The Savoy

The financial success of the Savoy enabled Richard D'Oyly Carte to buy other hotels, including Claridge's in 1894 (which he immediately rebuilt) and Rome's Grand Hotel in 1896, a bad bargain that he made at Ritz's urging.

In 1897 Carte dismissed Ritz and Escoffier, and their entire team left with them. Ritz and his *maître d'hôtel* Echenard had been implicated in the disappearance of over £3,400 (equivalent to nearly half a million pounds today) in wine and spirits, and Escoffier was accused of accepting sweeteners from suppliers. Despite the Victorians' reputation for probity, this was a time of daring deals where corners were often cut. In 1890 Carte had lost the services of Gilbert for three years after charging him, contrary to their agreement, one-third of the cost of recarpeting the theatre. Gilbert, a successful lawyer before turning librettist, sued Carte as other overcharges were discovered, including nearly £1,000 for electric lighting. The three men were reconciled eventually, but the last two Savoyard operas were mere shadows of their original successes.

Richard D'Oyly Carte died in 1901, having created a hotel and theatrical empire. Carte's son Rupert D'Oyly Carte became chairman of the Savoy hotel group in 1903 but Helen Carte, his stepmother and Richard's second wife, was the power behind the throne until her death in 1913.

Under Rupert the hotel was expanded across a dramatic land bridge over Carting Lane on to the Strand and past the Savoy Theatre. Both buildings thereby gained a splendid new entrance off the Strand where, by custom, carriages and – later – taxis were obliged to enter the Savoy's courtyard in the right-hand lane (as opposed to the left as found elsewhere in Britain). This anomaly allowed the driver to release the cab door with his right hand, thereby letting guests alight without the delay normally caused by a driver walking around his cab. It was yet another brilliant and distinctive innovation. Today the forecourt of the Savoy Hotel is the only place in Britain where vehicles drive on the right.

The taciturn Rupert also added the hotel's famous American Bar, a new Grill with dance floor (the Savoy was the first British hotel to offer music to diners) and a dance band called the Savoy Orpheans. The Savoy also created Britain's first serviced apartments that offered access to all the hotel's amenities. The actress Sarah Bernhardt was among those who lived at the Savoy for decades.

THE AMERICAN BAR

The American Bar at the Savoy has been in its current location since 1904 when Ada 'Coley' Coleman took over from Frank Wells, the first barman to serve cocktails at the Savoy. Coley invented the Hanky-Panky cocktail for actor Sir Charles Hawtrey, while Harry Craddock, who took over in 1925, invented the White Lady.

The bar itself remains a small counter just big enough for two mixologists at any one time, while guests are seated at tables around the white baby grand piano.

Most of the great celebrity drinkers have propped up the American Bar including Ernest Hemingway, Marlene Dietrich, the Burton-Taylors and Richard Harris. George Bernard Shaw, the man who claimed 'I am only a beer teetotaller, not a champagne teetotaller', also imbibed at the Savoy.

The Savoy, with its unique forecourt and theatre, remains London's most instantly recognisable hotel. With his emphasis on outward probity, Richard D'Oyly Carte might be shocked by the behaviour of some of the celebrities who have stayed here since, but he'd love the fact that the Savoy still attracts the biggest names.

THE CALEDONIAN, EDINBURGH (1903)
WALDORF ASTORIA EDINBURGH – THE CALEDONIAN

In the nineteenth century two train lines were built to connect the Scottish capital of Edinburgh with London. One, the North British, hugged the east coast of England while the other, the Caledonian, travelled along the west coast, arriving via Glasgow.

It went without saying that each train company would build a great hotel at its Edinburgh terminus. Railway hotels were not just profitable investments, they were fast becoming status symbols.

But the Caledonian Railway Company hit financial problems and didn't even complete its Princes Street station until 1903. The reason for this was the volatility of railway investment in those pioneering days. Fortunes were made – and lost – very quickly.

In the 1840s Sir William Tite, who had recently designed the Royal Exchange in London, designed a grand station to be sited just below Edinburgh Castle. The cost of building the line proved so expensive, however, that for the next twenty years passengers in the Caledonian's distinctive purple and white carriages would arrive to little more than a shed. In June 1890 this structure burned down, but fortuitously, fresh funds soon arrived from new lines across the Forth Rail Bridge. This injection of capital emboldened the directors to build first a grand station accessed through three Neoclassical arches and then a hotel on top of the station, which finally opened in 1903.

Because the hotel was built directly over the terminus, the station's three arches were incorporated into the hotel design. The one on the left led into reception. The middle arch became the manager's office and the third arch (today the hotel bar) led to the platforms. A very wide and grand staircase was built behind reception. Its size was necessary because the new Princes Street Hotel had no lift. All guests and all staff carrying luggage used these same busy five flights of stairs until the 1950s. For this reason the newly appointed architects, Peddie and Kinnear, created a 'privacy screen' on each floor, a form of glass and wood double glazing between the staircase and those bedrooms that faced on to it. This lessened the noise of boots on the stairs and when two guest lifts and a service lift were finally introduced after the Second World War, the screens remained.

Another unusual feature of the Princes Street Hotel was the way it followed the wedge-shaped floorplan of the station. Because of the encroachment of existing roads, the terminus, its seven platforms and hotel were located on two sides of a triangle with Rutland Street constraining it on the third.

Names are curious things and sometimes have a life of their own. Soon after its opening in 1903 this towering red structure in Dumfries sandstone gained an affectionate local nickname. It was never the Princes Street Hotel, nor even the Caledonian. Instead, posters in the city proclaimed, 'Come to the Caley for almost royal magnificence'.

When west coast trains ceased running into this station in 1965, the hotel took over the whole ground floor of the station. The old concourse leading to the platforms was roofed over and became a lofty, large palm-court style lounge. Since the Caley was taken over by Hilton and rebranded Waldorf Astoria in 2012, this lounge is now known as Peacock Alley (after the original Peacock Alley that ran between New York's Waldorf and Astoria hotels).

Competing with the much larger North British Hotel (now the Balmoral), the Caley always had to aim high. Its telegraphic address was simply 'Luxury Edinburgh' and its Louis XIV drawing room (now the Pompadour Restaurant) on the entresol was positively regal in décor. The head porter, Henry Plesch, spoke eight languages including Russian, which was helpful in assigning rooms when in 1909 Tsar Nicholas II sent Count Bobinsky and Duma President Honyakoff to Edinburgh to negotiate loans for the Russian government.

Although King George V had a palace nearby at Holyrood, his son the playboy Prince of Wales was often a visitor at the Caley. In 1937 after he had become King Edward VIII, the hotel made headlines around the world when veteran doorman Sandy James was asked by an American guest what he thought about the Abdication Crisis. To his surprise Mr James soon found his words quoted in the *New York Times* and the *Washington Post* with the advice that, 'Anybody who wants a reliable summary of public opinion in the United Kingdom should immediately contact the doorman of the Caledonian Hotel in Edinburgh, Scotland'.

While the Caley continued to attract wealthy and titled visitors in the 1930s and 40s, it was the new Edinburgh Festival that confirmed it as the celebrity hotel of choice. This lengthy international festival of the arts began nearby in 1947. In its first few years Laurence Olivier, Sir Malcolm

Sargent, Dame Margot Fonteyn, Alec Guinness, and Sir John Barbirolli all stayed at the Caley. Celebrity cowboy Roy Rogers also slept here with his horse Trigger, which he famously led up the stairs to their room. (When the photographers were gone, Trigger was smuggled out quietly and taken to a nearby stable for the night.)

BILLY GARIOCH

A number of suites at the Caledonian have been named after Scottish luminaries such as Sir Walter Scott, Robert Louis Stevenson, and telephone pioneer, Sir Alexander Graham Bell. But there is also one that commemorates Billy Garioch, who worked for the Caley for 50 years, first as a page boy and eventually becoming Head of Baggage.

Billy was a firm favourite with many of the stars, including Burt Lancaster, who used to tip him a princely 2/6d whenever Billy carried his golf clubs to the car. Billy's favourite guest, however, was Nelson Mandela who in 1997 attended the Commonwealth Heads of Government Conference. The South African president insisted on shaking the hands of everyone who was going to be looking after him. No guest had ever done this before. The normally teetotal Mandela also drank whisky from a traditional silver quaich presented to him at the hotel by the Lord Provost of Edinburgh, and then declared, 'I'm going to the conference now. I hope I won't be too aggressive'.

Over the years very few celebrities visiting Edinburgh have

failed to stay at the Caley; those who have include Laurel and Hardy, Sean Connery, Queen Salote of Tonga and Clint Eastwood. In 1953 Jack Kerkes, the hotel joiner, told the story of making an extra-large bed for the extra-large queen. Jack later adapted that same bed for Clint's six-foot four-inch frame.

The three-arched hotel is still immediately recognisable from photographs of the building of 1903, although life within is far less formal now. Even in 1966 men in jeans or without a tie would be followed round by the head porter until they left. On one occasion a page called Billy Garioch was sent out to bar the entrance of a scruffy pair who had driven up to the front door. 'He had a pair of jeans on and an old donkey jacket that was ripped at the side. I was supposed to go and ask them to leave, but as I approached them, she unveiled her face. My heart stopped. It was Liz Taylor. The man she was with was Richard Burton.'

THE WALDORF HOTEL, LONDON (1908)
THE WALDORF HILTON LONDON

The Waldorf Hotel on Aldwych was conceived as an American-style venture to rival the Savoy. It even took the name of the wealthiest American alive, William Waldorf Astor.

From 1889 a curving site on the western rim of Aldwych had been reserved for a hotel that would be constructed between two new theatres, the Waldorf and Aldwych. In due course Edward Sanders, a theatrical impresario, hired Alexander Marshall Mackenzie – brother-in-law of the distinguished designer Charles Rennie Mackintosh – to be its architect. As the Scotsman had never designed a hotel before, he sailed to Manhattan to study the new style.

The design that Mackenzie came back with used a central Grand Court (now the hotel's Palm Court) with a series of major public rooms running off on three sides of it, and retail units to the front facing onto Aldwych. There would also be a dining room, a grill and a bar on the ground floor. One American innovation that both the Aldwych and the Savoy embraced was opening the hotel not just for guests but for passers-by who could call in for dinner, afternoon tea or a drink.

Mackenzie had specified a steel skeleton, which meant that the hotel – with its unbroken 190-foot curving façade of Aberdeen granite, brick and Portland stone – could be constructed in only eighteen months.

When it opened in January 1908, London's new West End hotel had nearly 400 bedrooms and 176 bathrooms. This was considered 'ample bath accommodation' according to the London press of the day. Indeed the 1911 *Baedeker Guide to London* noted that 'the number of bathrooms is said to be proportionately larger than in any other hotel in the world'. This was not true – the Savoy offered 268 bedrooms, of which more than 200 were en suite – but it was still impressive.

Among other American innovations were electric lights that could be switched off from the bedside and a telephone in every bedroom. And there were three lifts (still in situ today), two for residents and one for luggage.

For the gentlemen there was a smoking room on the ground floor and a billiard room on the first. For the ladies there was a first-floor writing room (now known as the Aldwych Suite) which was decorated in rose pink wallpaper.

Mackenzie's design was modular, allowing for suites to be created by linking bedrooms. There were also chambermaid rooms and boot-brushing rooms on each floor to service the

Photo: Edward/Gallery

rooms. The Waldorf was set up not just to attract diners and overnight guests, but, as at the Savoy, permanent residents whose custom would guarantee a regular income.

THE ASTOR FAMILY

The Waldorf Hotel, like the theatre next door, was named after William Waldorf Astor (1848–1919) whose cousin and rival John Jacob Astor IV built the Astoria on New York's Fifth Avenue in 1897. In fact John Jacob pointedly built his hotel next to cousin William's hotel and made it four storeys taller.

After falling out with his American relatives, William Waldorf Astor moved to London where he owned the *Observer* newspaper and eventually secured a peerage. He was a remarkably secretive man. The extent of his involvement in the Waldorf Hotel is unclear. Whether the future Viscount Astor financed the whole project, bailed out the original entrepreneurs, or simply lent his prestigious name may never be known.

The new hotel soon joined Claridge's, the Ritz, and the Savoy as one of London's great society hotels. Affluent Londoners who had recently taken up the New York model of entertaining friends and colleagues in hotels threw elaborate parties at the Waldorf. At one such event in 1913 the scandalous new 'Creole Tango' was danced in a London hotel for the first time.

In 1915 the Great War came very close to the Waldorf when a German zeppelin raid hit Aldwych, killing 200 people, but just missing the hotel. (This near-miss happened again during the Second World War; a study of where bombs landed in both wars suggests that the curved frontage of the Waldorf made it difficult to target.)

After the Great War, London's West End embarked on a period of deliberate frivolity. Newspapers of the day wrote of people 'frivolling at the Waldorf'. In 1926 Howard Godfrey became the leader of 'The Waldorfians', the hotel's resident orchestra. Another coup for Godfrey was to make fifteen 78rpm discs 'recorded live at the Waldorf' with Al Bowlly before the singer emigrated to the United States in 1934.

The outbreak of the Second World War posed a number of challenges to the Waldorf. Initially many of its wealthy patrons fled the capital to stay in hotels like the Imperial in Torquay while the expected destruction of London took place. The hotel countered by placing advertisements in the press reassuring customers that its alloy structure made it safe in the event of Luftwaffe attacks on the capital. (The Dorchester followed suit, insisting that its basements were bomb-proof.) But the promised Blitzkrieg was delayed and during the 'phoney war' the hotel's regulars returned. When the Blitz began in earnest most stayed on.

One of the strangest events of the Waldorf's war occurred in 1941 when the British Secret Service rented room 519 to interrogate Stella Lonsdale, an English woman freshly arrived from Marseille. Stella claimed to be a double agent and wanted British help to return under cover to unoccupied France. Although the telephone in her room was bugged – and she dined regularly and indiscreetly with her MI5 handlers for a month – operatives failed to verify or disprove her story. They were also shocked by her sexually explicit conversations and at the bill she ran up at the Waldorf's grill. Eventually she was imprisoned for withholding information helpful to the war effort.

During the nightly blackouts the West End became a dangerous place. In 1944 one well-dressed rogue, known in the press as the Monocled Gunman, seized the contents of the till from the Waldorf's receptionist and fired two shots in the air before running out of the hotel into Aldwych.

After the war the hotel was, like most of Britain, almost bankrupt and struggling to find its place in the world. At the Waldorf this sense of disorientation was epitomised in the sad case of head waiter Alphonse Marceau. In 1947 he fell ill. Alphonse had worked at the Waldorf since it opened in 1908 and for sixteen of those years he hadn't even taken a holiday, so great was his love of the hotel. Obliged to retire early because of ill-health, he committed suicide – by throwing himself under a train – rather than live without his beloved Waldorf.

In 1958 the restaurateur Charles Forte bought the hotel for £800,000. The Waldorf was the first of more than 800 hotels that Forte was to fold into his empire and by the 1960s it had regained its position at the centre of London life.

In 2004 the Hilton Corporation was brought in to run the Waldorf and eventually created Waldorf-Astoria as its premiere brand, reuniting the names of the two American cousins who a hundred years before had vied to create the best hotels in New York.

THE DORCHESTER, LONDON (1931)

The Dorchester sits like a section of some great 1930s luxury liner moored on London's Park Lane. On the outside it is a broad sweep of Art Deco curves and ocean-going metal balconies, while on the inside its gilded lobby and main concourse, the Promenade, spends £5,000 a week on flowers. This is *Le Style Dorchester.*

Today the hotel is something of a showbusiness institution, but during the Second World War it was the epicentre of West End war fever. Here in 1943 and 1944, as the conflict turned in the Allies' favour, generals met their mistresses, members of the British government sat out Luftwaffe raids and Ernest Hemingway moved rapidly from wife number three to wife number four.

Built in 1931, the hotel rose up on the site of the old Dorchester House opposite a pair of gates into Hyde Park. Dorchester House had been the grandest of all the mansions on Park Lane. It was constructed in 1853 by the hugely wealthy MP, Robert Stayner Holford. In 1929 Gordon Hotels and the McAlpine company drew up plans to demolish the mansion and create what they claimed would the 'perfect' modern hotel.

The partnership intended to combine the latest ideas in modern design with all the conveniences of modern technology. This new venture was not without its critics, however. Even in 1900 there had been grumblings in the London press that aristocratic Park Lane was beginning to resemble New York's Fifth Avenue. The Dorchester, with its pared-down architectural lines, sealed that peripheral road's reputation for glamour and fast living.

The structure was built using reinforced concrete which allowed for the creation of huge internal spaces without supporting pillars. Forty thousand tons of earth were excavated to create an unprecedentedly large basement. Even today one-third of the hotel remains invisible below ground, with waiters using escalators to get food to restaurant tables in time.

Photo: UggBoy

Also hidden away in the Dorchester is a nineteenth-century octagonal oak-panelled salon. The Byford Room, close to the current ballroom, is one of several sections of the original Dorchester House that were incorporated and built around rather than demolished.

From its opening in 1931 the Dorchester attracted the rich and the famous. Despite hosting a raft of visiting movie stars from Hollywood, the majority of its celebrity clientele has always been British. Writers like Cecil Day-Lewis and W. Somerset Maugham, and artists like Sir Cecil Beaton and Sir Alfred Munnings were regulars in the 1930s.

In 1938 the Dorchester pulled off a coup, poaching Harry Craddock, the most famous barman in Britain, from the Savoy's American Bar. Craddock celebrated with 'The Dorchester of London', a new cocktail combining gin, Bacardi and Forbidden Fruit (a liquor that smells like honey but tastes like a liquorice grapefruit) to mark the occasion. Recently an original bottle of Forbidden Fruit was tracked down and the cocktail is once again available at the Dorchester.

During the Second World War the Dorchester's proximity to all the important embassies, and Sir Robert McAlpine's claims for its bomb-proof construction, made it hugely popular with correspondents, diplomats and spies. Lord Halifax, the British Foreign Secretary, took over eight rooms at the Dorchester – until he was sent to Washington as US ambassador – and General Dwight D. Eisenhower took rooms on the first floor (now the Eisenhower Suite) which became his headquarters in the months running up to D-Day.

In May 1944 Ernest Hemingway, who had been sitting out the conflict on a fishing boat in Cuba, flew to London to become a war correspondent. In a rather underhanded deal with his wife's publishers, he appropriated her commission – and her seat on a plane across the Atlantic. Mrs Hemingway, the young but formidable journalist Martha Gellhorn, was left to make the crossing slowly on a supply ship full of explosives, the only method of transportation available.

Hemingway quickly made himself at home in Harry Craddock's bar where he bought drinks for RAF pilots whose exploits over Germany he wanted to report. By then, with D-Day imminent, the West End was nothing but one long party for those who could afford it. Hemingway was frequently very drunk indeed. On 24 May his car crashed in the blackout and the writer ended up at St George's Hospital, on the other side of Hyde Park Corner, with a lot of stitches in his head.

When Martha Gellhorn arrived from the States on 31 May, she found Hem throwing a party in his hospital room instead of recuperating quietly. She finished with him on the spot.

Hemingway's story is typical of the Dorchester. Big names have a tendency do big things in this hotel. Elizabeth Taylor read the script of *Cleopatra* – or the contract, or both – in her bath in the Harlequin Suite, the most expensive of three new suites added in the 1960s. A pink marble bathroom was installed at her request ahead of her visit. It's been preserved exactly as it was on the day that she signed Hollywood's first million-dollar contract. In fact the hotel is not allowed to change the bath, making it one of the very few 'listed baths' in Britain.

Taylor's husband, Richard Burton, preferred to stay in the overblown Oliver Messel Suite, designed in the 1950s by Messel, the leading theatrical designer of his time. It resembles the interior of a Georgian country house, but not necessarily in a good way. In 1978 Burton gave a press conference for the film *The Wild Geese* in this suite, a bottle of whisky on the table in front of him.

FILM DIRECTORS AT THE DORCHESTER

The director Alfred Hitchcock always insisted on a suite with one of the best views of Hyde Park, explaining to staff that the Dorchester was a perfect place for a murder because there was so much space nearby for burying the body.

Like Hitchcock, the director David Lean used his suite at the Dorchester for auditions. In 1940 Deborah Kerr met with Lean who was the editor on Gabriel Pascal's film of *Major Barbara*. 'How bizarre it was,' she later wrote. 'This room full of chaps smoking enormous cigars and drinking martinis and this young girl reciting the Lord's Prayer.'

Many celebrity writers have also entered the Dorchester because of its long tradition of hosting Foyle's Literary Lunches. One of the least successful was given in 1964 when John Lennon was invited to say something about his book of surreal stories and drawings, *In his own Write*. Hungover and propped up by his wife Cynthia, Lennon was only able to mutter, 'Thank you very much, it's been a pleasure'.

Although Nelson Mandela was feted at the Dorchester on the eve of the unveiling of his statue on Parliament Square in 2007, the hotel has always been more of a place for showbusiness types than statesmen. One American singer (whose name has still not been divulged) paid to have his suite redecorated to resemble a nightclub so that he could continue to entertain friends every evening after performing in the West End.

The Dorchester has always been famously and frustratingly discreet, but does not shy away from extravagant gestures of its own. The Crystal Suite function room contains a glittering piano covered in mirrored mosaic tiles, one of two that used to belong to Liberace. The other one belongs to the almost equally flamboyant Sir Elton John. That is the kind of place the Dorchester is.

THE MIDLAND HOTEL, MORECAMBE (1933)

By the end of the nineteenth century the world's railway companies were some of the most prolific builders of hotels. Taking their cue from the grand hotels of Europe and America, they produced statement buildings like the soaring Midland Grand Hotel, built as the gateway to London's St Pancras station, and which remains one of the most impressive Neo-Gothic buildings in Britain. In Genoa the Grand Hotel Savoia was originally a terminus hotel; so were the Railway Hotel Hua Hin, Thailand, and the Royal York in Toronto.

After the First World War the railway hotel went into a slow decline as more and more wealthy people began travelling long-distance in their own motor cars. One of the last gasps of the station hotel as a building intended to communicate prestige was in the Lancashire seaside resort of Morecambe, perhaps best known today as the birthplace of the British comedian Eric Morecambe.

In 1933 when young Eric – then John Eric Bartholomew – was seven years old, the Midland Hotel in Morecambe was demolished and a new 48-bedroom Midland Hotel in a chic, geometric European style known as International (or Streamline Moderne) was unveiled. The eye-catching design was by Oliver Hill, who had been commissioned by the London, Midland and Scottish Railways company. Hill's low, curving white palace on the seashore created a sensation and the press showered rave reviews on the architect. Hill had spared none of his client's money, employing the sculptor Eric Gill, the painter Eric Ravilious and the American textile designer Marion Dorn for the interiors.

The decision to go for broke in Morecambe had been made by the LMS's Controller of Hotels, Arthur Towle. Towle had recently also employed Sir Edwin Lutyens to design an annex for the company's Midland Hotel in Manchester and it is possible that Lutyens recommended Hill.

Ironically, Hill was only a recent convert to Modernism, having discovered the style on a visit to Stockholm. In Morecambe he indulged its bright linear logic to the full, creating a light, airy central lobby with, rising above it, a beautiful circular staircase topped by an Eric Gill medallion of Poseidon and naked sea nymphs. Gill also created other carvings, including a relief map of northwest England dominated by a central white image of the hotel for the wall of one of the function rooms. From the lobby two long curving wings extended north and south over three floors. A circular glass tea room with a mural by Ravilious stood at the northern end. Unique circular rugs and floor mosaics were created by Dorn while the whole building was covered in a white render called Snowcrete that could be polished to resemble marble. Its flat, parapeted roof, not overlooked by any building in Morecambe, was designed for exclusive sunbathing. In July 1933 the Earl of Derby opened the hotel and thereafter black-tie dinner-dances were held every Saturday evening with dancing to Orlando's Band. This was a level of opulence not seen before on the north-west coast of Britain.

Perhaps not surprisingly the Midland quickly became a destination hotel in its own right. The smart set drove up from London to stay in a hotel that ostensibly served railway passengers. If the hotel lost touch with its railway roots, this only presaged the great change that was to sweep Britain after the Second World War when many railways lines were axed, cars became generally affordable and motorways speeded up road travel.

FAMOUS GUESTS

In the days when Morecambe attracted big-name entertainers, the Midland was first choice to host the top-billed artistes, including the singers Alma Cogan and Max Bygraves, the comedians Abbot and Costello, and Tommy Trinder. In 1959 Laurence Olivier stayed at the hotel while making the film version of John Osborne's *The Entertainer* in Morecambe's Winter Gardens. Olivier received an Academy Best Actor nomination in 1960 for his performance as the seedy entertainer Archie Rice.

In 1952 the Hotels Executive of Britain's nationalised railways company sold off the Midland, as it did many of its hotels in the 1950s. The Midland did not thrive. The advent of the cheap package holiday to the Mediterranean was making UK seaside hotels an unappealing investment.

The poor Midland was repeatedly relaunched and modernised. Contemporary signage, flock wallpaper and floral carpets obscured everything that had made the hotel stylish and unique. On Hill's daring exterior, a long advert

Photo: English Lakes Hotels and The Midland

for rooms starting at £9.99 obscured the beautiful glass and Snowcrete stairwell. The hotel stood empty and vandalised for ten years in the 1980s, and one of Eric Gill's bas reliefs was chipped off and stolen – though it was later recovered.

Then in 1989 the Midland was used as a location for an episode of the popular TV detective series *Poirot*. 'Double Sin' was originally going to be filmed on the south coast of England, but the discovery of a hotel that matched the Art Deco world of London Weekend Television's drama series inspired the producers to rewrite the storyline. Poirot was sent north and when 'Double Sin' was aired, many people were amazed to find that such a building still existed in Britain.

In 1998 the fate of the Midland Hotel – like that of so many grand hotels – hung in the balance, with demolition one option and conversion into luxury flats the other. Fortunately in 2003 it was bought by Urban Splash, a UK property regeneration company who restored it and took the hotel back to its 1930s original. Apart from a series of six discreet penthouses on the roof, the building now looks exactly as it once did to those approaching from the railway station. The public rooms are once again graced with the decorative features of Gill, Dorn, and Ravilious. The circular tea room is now the Rotunda Bar, and the dining room is now a secondary bar, reflecting changes in British drinking habits. The only change to the original footprint is the new dining room that has been created out of a 1950s glass sun lounge on the sea side of the hotel. This had been added to Hill's design in 1955, but it's now been sympathetically incorporated into the structure to look as if it were part of the original design. Passers-by on the promenade can now see guests seated at dinner – an unthinkable violation of privacy in the 1930s – but this once again reflects changing attitudes to hotels. Patrons no longer expect 1930s levels of seclusion.

The whole restoration project cost £11 million and is a remarkable achievement that is also bringing tourists back to Morecambe. So many beautiful hotels were lost in the twentieth century, it is a cause for rejoicing that the Midland was not just restored as a building, but restored as a destination in its own right.

FRANCE

LE MEURICE, PARIS (1835)

No hotel in Paris has as long a history as Le Meurice. The man who created it was Charles Augustin Meurice, who in 1771 was a postmaster in Calais. In that year Monsieur Meurice had the idea of setting up a hotel in the English Channel port.

Business was soon disrupted by decades of wars between France and England but in 1815 Meurice opened a second hotel, this time in Paris's Rue Saint-Honoré. (His original Hôtel Meurice is still there in Calais but it was rebuilt in 1954.) Meurice, then in his late 70s, knew that if he put his two hotels at the service of the wary English gent who arrived in Calais with no French currency and little command of the language, he would soon make himself invaluable. It was said in the 1820s that the only word of French that an Englishman needed on arrival in France was 'Meurice!' The twin hotels would take care of everything else.

In 1835 the Paris Meurice relocated one city block closer to the Jardin des Tuileries, at its current location on the Rue de Rivoli, but its carriage entrance and lobby were built at the back, on the much quieter Rue de Mont Thabor. With easy access to the Louvre and the opera houses, Le Meurice became home for generations of wealthy Francophiles of all nations. The poet Léon-Paul Fargue famously divided visitors to his city into three categories: 'poor, good, and of the Meurice.'

Among those for whom Le Meurice was good enough was Queen Victoria. In 1855 she became the first British monarch to enter the capital of England's ancient enemy in 400 years. Peter Ilych Tchaikovsky also stayed at Le Meurice when visiting Paris in February 1876. One night he went to hear *Carmen* at the Opéra-Comique and wrote enthusiastically from the hotel to his benefactor, Nadezhda von Meck: '*Carmen* is a masterpiece in every sense of the word!'

By 1865 Le Meurice had been taken over by the London and Paris Hotel Company, with Henri-Joseph Scheurich as its proprietor and manager. Scheurich was still managing in 1891, by which time the hotel, with its Louis XVI furniture, had begun tentatively to embrace electric lighting and en suite plumbing. The famed Meurice was about to be knocked off its perch, however. In June 1898 César Ritz's new hotel on Place Vendôme opened. Suddenly Paris had a new shining star that attracted royalty just as much as it attracted wealthy tourists.

A number of investors got together to aid Le Meurice, including another veteran Swiss hotelier, Frédéric Schwenter. Schwenter and his partners opted to enlarge the hotel by merging it with Le Metropole on Rue de Castiglione. They employed the architect Henri Paul Nénot, a recent winner of the Grand Prix de Rome, for a comprehensive modernisation and rebuild that left only the façades untouched. By 1908 a roof garden restaurant had arisen on the seventh floor and this, with its unbeatable view across Paris, became the place for French society to dine. (Its terrace was used by Woody Allen as a glamorous location for his 2011 film *Midnight in Paris*.)

In the early decades of the twentieth century the excellence of Le Meurice drew in a brilliant and eccentric range of guests, from the spy and dancer Mata Hari – who paid her bills so infrequently that the manager once obtained a court

order against her – to the exiled King Alfonso XIII of Spain who after being dethroned sought refuge at Le Meurice and set up his government-in-exile there. The poet, politician and all-round self-publicist Gabriele D'Annunzio also stayed at Le Meurice, as did Count Galeazzo Ciano, Mussolini's son-in-law and foreign minister. Surrealists like Giorgio de Chirico and Salvador Dalí were among the artists who were easily satisfied with the best.

DALÍ AND THE SHEEP

For 30 years, the Surrealist painter Salvador Dalí tried to spend a month each year at Le Meurice in a suite spanning Rooms 102 and 103. He was known to give autographed lithographs of his work to staff in lieu of Christmas tips. Dalí lived up to his reputation for eccentricity. He once asked the staff to capture flies from the Tuileries Garden, paying them a generous fee of five francs for each. On another occasion he asked room service for a flock of sheep to be brought up to his room. When this was done he fired blanks from a pistol at them.

Dalí often made use of sheep in his 'installations'. While staying in Los Angeles he begged his wealthy hosts for two sheep which he raised off the ground in harnesses while an actress declaimed poetry and threw bread at the audience.

During the Second World War this calm and understated hotel was commandeered as the residence of the last German governor of Paris, Dietrich von Choltitz, who had a suite overlooking the Tuileries. Here in 1944 he famously received – and ignored – an order from Adolf Hitler to blow up the city. Later, on 25 August, Von Choltitz surrendered to French troops in that same suite.

Le Meurice has always been a favourite hotel of heads of state, from Franklin D. Roosevelt to the Shah of Iran and the Bey of Tunis. Its guest book was a *Who's Who* of Hollywood long before the Burton-Taylors took up occasional residence in the 1960s.

The hotel has made a point of changing very little. The only major alterations occurred in 1997–2000 when the main entrance was finally – after 135 years – moved round to the more glamorous Rue de Rivoli, and again in 2007 when, under the direction of designer Philippe Starck and general manager Franka Holtmann, the ground floor was refurbished with an extraordinary level of decorative panache. A restaurant named Le Dalí after the sheep-shooter of Room 103 was created under a massive ceiling canvas painted by Philippe Starck's daughter, Ara Starck.

But continuity is the core of Le Meurice, and deliberately so. From early in its nineteenth-century history, the visual style of the hotel has remained the same: Louis XVI with an understated livery of celadon and taupe. To this the twentieth century added an unusual coat of arms featuring two greyhounds, a tribute to a stray dog that took up residence with the builders during the renovations of 1907 and became a hotel mascot. Today bedroom lights are still worked by switches – no iPads or sensors here – and if you want coffee in the morning you have to ring room service. The relentless march of Nespresso machines has not reached this discreet hotel on the Rue de Rivoli, not yet and maybe never.

GRAND HÔTEL TERMINUS, PARIS (1889)
HILTON PARIS OPERA

At the time of Paris' first great Exposition Universelle in 1855, Napoleon III realised his capital offered a few exclusive gentlemanly hotels like Le Meurice but hardly any large comfortable hotels for the middle classes. With more exhibitions planned, the new emperor urged Parisians to build bigger. The first hotel to answer his request was Grand Hôtel du Louvre with its 700 rooms and steam-powered lifts (1855), then came the Grand Hôtel de Paris with its 750 bedrooms (1867) and finally the Hôtel Continental, opened under the Third Republic for the third Exposition Universelle of 1878.

With a fourth World Fair coming up in 1889, Paris looked for inspiration to Britain where architects had pioneered a new kind of hotel attached to railway stations. These huge structures combined comfort, economy of scale, and direct access to city centres without having to take one's carriage through miles of suburbs. London's first station hotel had been the relatively modest Great Northern Hotel at King's Cross (1854) but since then the Grosvenor and Charing Cross hotels, both in the fashionable French chateau style, had demonstrated how practical and profitable these structures could be.

The initiative for Paris's first integrated railway hotel came from the Compagnie des Chemins de Fer de l'Ouest who ran trains as far as Normandy from their brand-new Saint-Lazare station. The hotel was to be located directly in front of the station, partly masking its façade.

The architect was a distinguished engineer called Émile Lavezzari (1832–1887) who set off for several months researching English and Spanish railway hotels. Unfortunately Laverazzi died in July 1887 before the first stone was even laid. His project was handed over to Jean Juste Gustave Lisch (1828 –1910), a skilled designer of railway stations who had just completed Gare Saint-Lazare, which the hotel would now obscure. Because the next World Fair was imminent, he managed to complete the Grand Hôtel Terminus in just fifteen months at a cost of 12 million francs.

The Terminus opened on 7 May 1889, the day after the opening of the Exposition Universelle itself. Gustave Eiffel's tower was opened eight days later (with its lifts still not functioning).

A story runs that President of France Marie François Sadi Carnot visited and was shown round by Lisch, expressing great interest in the 18-metre glass and metal bridge that connected Gare Saint-Lazare over Rue Intérieure to the hotel. Once inside a double flight of stairs ran down into the hotel lobby. The hotel's great boast was that patrons would be met on the platform and escorted to their room across this bridge while their luggage was brought through by porters. Within five minutes of a train arriving, guests would be in their bedrooms.

At the bottom of the great double staircase two lions stood guarding a reading room full of massive tables. This lobby (currently known as Le Grand Salon) rose the height of three floors and was decorated with chandeliers, frescoes and colonnades like the inside of a Venetian palazzo. Upper balconies allowed visiting ladies to observe the comings and goings below. Sadly these magnificent staircases were removed in a subsequent renovation when the hotel was separated from the station, but you can still see that one of the original cherubs on the uppermost frieze is showing his bottom to the hotel. This is said to be a result of the artist

Charles Joseph Lameire falling out with the railway company and making his feelings felt in a subtle way.

From this reading room elevators rose to six floors containing 500 bedrooms. Given that the hotel now has only 268 rooms, they must have been minute. One of the hotel's many electrical innovations was a bedroom key that when turned, dimmed the main light and brought up the bedside lamps.

Despite a bomb attack in 1894 by the anarchist Émile Henry, the Terminus quickly proved very popular with Parisians as well as visitors. The hotel had its own grocery store, Caves et Comestibles (where the restaurant Pain Quotidien now stands). Here passengers travelling west from Saint-Lazare could stock up for the provinces.

CLAUDE MONET

In 1883 the artist Claude Monet began living in Giverny with his wife. He had seen the picturesque village from the train while travelling on the Chemins de Fer de l'Ouest line. Eventually in 1890 Monet bought the house whose garden, lake and water lilies he painted repeatedly.

When he came to Paris, the painter would often stay at Hôtel Terminus for two or three weeks at a time. The great advantage of the station was that he could arrive in his country clothes, cross the bridge and change into his city clothes in his bedroom while porters unloaded his baggage.

Monet painted eleven pictures of Gare Saint-Lazare and continued to divide his time between Paris and the house with the pink façade and famous garden until his death in 1926.

Some people became long-term guests of Hôtel Terminus, including the farceur Georges Feydeau. In 1909 when his wife decided to move a little further out of town, Feydeau moved into the hotel for a week. He ended up staying ten years in Room 189 until there was no longer any space to hang all the artworks he had bought locally (including some Van Goghs). The actors and directors of Paris theatres would visit the sullen playwright in his room. His desk was often so full of books and papers that he wrote on a board that covered the bidet.

In the 1930s, despite a world crisis hitting the French hotel business, the Grand Hôtel Terminus embarked on an extensive period of renovation. The designer Henri Pacon, known for his work on ocean-going liners and the remodelling of Gare de Caen for Compagnie des Chemins de Fer de l'Ouest, was commissioned to update the ground floor. Pacon introduced an auditorium, turned the *table d'hôte* restaurant into a billiard room, created a tasting bar for oysters and shellfish, and established the brand-new Café Terminus on Rue Saint-Lazare where Parisians could dance to the hotel's jazz orchestra.

The party ended when Paris was occupied during the Second World War but the hotel played its part in the Resistance. While German officers were entertained upstairs in the billiard room, down in the basement a tunnel that led under Rue Intérieure enabled Resistance fighters to access train platforms and head in and out of Paris without having to show their papers at the Ausweis checkpoint.

In November 1944 after the liberation of Paris the hotel was requisitioned by the American Red Cross and renamed 'Grand Central Club'. It served 628,000 meals in one year to troops and refugees.

In 1973, Guy Taittinger, oldest son of Pierre Taittinger the champagne-maker, bought the tired-looking Terminus and made it part of his Concorde Hotels, as Hôtel Concorde Saint-Lazare. It passed to the Blackstone Group in 2013 and, after a lengthy restoration that revealed and restored the exceptional beauty of the old reading room, it reopened as the Paris Opera Hilton in 2015.

THE RITZ, PARIS (1898)

César Ritz wasn't the first hotelier to name a hotel after himself – Giuseppe 'Danieli' da Niel, Charles Augustin Meurice and Eduard Sacher beat him to that – but he's the only hotelier whose name became an adjective: 'Ritzy'.

Ritz, like many celebrated hoteliers, was Swiss but he was a strange, driven man, even by the obsessive standards of most general managers. In the late nineteenth century he more than anyone raised the social status of the hotel to unheard-of heights by his attention to detail, his ability to anticipate his guests' every need and to exceed their expectations; and, not least, his ability to schmooze. Discreet and charming, Ritz had better contacts than many kings and presidents. He also worked himself extremely hard, managing several of Europe's first-rate establishments – fourteen at one point – simultaneously. In 1902 he had a nervous breakdown after the coronation of Edward VII of England was postponed by two months. This small delay wrecked Ritz's launch of London's new Carlton Hotel and he simply could not cope. The man who had lived his life in serene control of the pleasure palaces of Europe spent his last decade in a sanatorium not wishing to speak to anyone. He died in 1918 at the age of 68.

Today Ritz's memorials are his hotels, most notably the Ritz in Paris which he created, and the Savoy in London which he, even more than Richard D'Oyly Carte, established as a meeting place for aristocrats and royalty.

In 1889 the 39-year-old Ritz was running Grand Hôtel Monaco, Grand Hôtel National in Lucerne, and the Hôtel de Provence in Cannes when he was lured to the Savoy. Here with the assistance of his *chef de cuisine* Escoffier, the support of Lady de Grey and the patronage of the Prince of Wales, he convinced London society that the Savoy was an acceptable venue for mixed dining and entertaining in public. Ritz stayed nine years at the Savoy during which time he was also, at different times, running hotels in Frankfurt, Monte Carlo, Biarritz, Lucerne and Palermo as well as the Grand Hotel in Rome. Ritz's wife Marie-Louise wrote that during these years her husband's suitcases were never completely unpacked.

Then in 1897, Ritz and his partners were dismissed from the Savoy. Exactly what happened was never made public, but the kindest interpretation is that Ritz wasn't concentrating on the Savoy to the extent that D'Oyly Carte wanted and financial irregularities occurred. The singer Nellie Melba, among others, noted that Ritz's hitherto razor-sharp attention was often elsewhere. This was not surprising, as by May 1896 Ritz had already founded his Ritz Hotel Syndicate Ltd with five members of his Savoy team lined up to transfer allegiances. Now in his mid-forties, the *roi des hôteliers* was looking to outshine the Savoy with a new hotel of his own. Among his financial backers were the Armenian oil magnate Calouste Gulbenkian and Alfred Beit, the South African diamond millionaire. Ritz wasn't aiming at London, not yet. He had already optioned a site off Place Vendôme in Paris using money from Alexandre

Marnier-Lapostolle, manufacturer of Grand Marnier.

Place Vendôme suited Ritz well because he could retain the existing building's seventeenth-century façade while constructing a modern hotel that – unlike the Savoy – wouldn't look like one. His chosen architect, Charles-Frédéric Mewès, urged rooms with classic French interior designs (from Louis XIV to the First Empire). Although Ritz admitted that he did not understand design, he responded enthusiastically to Mewès' idea that their hotel should have a timeless beauty.

One stipulation Ritz made was that there should be no large lobby (as was common at the time). He believed large lobbies encouraged 'loiterers'. He also insisted on fitted cupboards because free-standing wardrobes gathered dust. On the day of the opening, 1 June 1898, Ritz decided the hotel's dining tables were a few centimetres too high so they were all packed off to the manufacturer to be cut down in time for the opening that evening.

Ritz was the obsessives' obsessive.

The opening was a great success, with the Rothschilds out 'en masse' according to Madame Ritz's account. Afterwards she and her husband stood by the Napoleonic column in Place Vendôme and talked all night about the future. 'This will be our daughter,' Ritz declared proudly.

But César Ritz's domination of the hotel world was about to be cut short. His next big project was to open the Carlton in London but the shock postponement of Edward VII's coronation precipitated a nervous breakdown. He had a second collapse in 1903 and Marie-Louise Ritz took over running their hotel. The great César Ritz died in a Swiss sanatorium just before the end of the First World War.

The years between the world wars were a time of almost impossible glamour at the Ritz. Elsa Maxwell hosted many parties, including one for the British Foreign Secretary Arthur Balfour, after which he thanked her 'for the most delightful and degrading evening I have ever spent'. Rudolf Valentino, Coco Chanel, Mary Pickford and the Rockefellers all stayed and dined. Harold Nicolson met Proust at the Ritz and found the author 'talkative but eccentric, dining in his fur coat and white gloves'. Scott Fitzgerald brought the young, impoverished Ernest Hemingway to drink at the Ritz. Cole Porter claimed he spent up to nine hours in the Ritz Bar every day and wrote 'Begin the Beguine' there.

In 1940 when Paris surrendered to the German army, the Ritz stayed open, using the rationale that it would be requisitioned anyway so might as well take the Wehrmacht's money. High-ranking officers who had done meritorious service were rewarded with a night or two at the famous Ritz. In the summer of 1940 Herman Goering arrived, allegedly to oversee the bombing of England before Hitler's invasion. He stayed in the Imperial Suite, which had been vacated only a few months before by Winston Churchill. It is said that Goering dressed in women's clothes and took a lot of drugs while in residence. Whether these distractions contributed to the Luftwaffe's failure to beat the RAF during the Battle of Britain is unclear.

On 25 August 1944 the Allies entered Paris. Hemingway, by now a famous novelist and epic carouser, followed closely behind as a war correspondent. Of course he claimed to have personally 'liberated' the hotel, but actually he drank first at the Travellers Club and then Café de la Paix. By the time he rolled up to the Ritz, the Germans were gone and other journalists had beaten him to it. Aware of Hem's Parisian progress, the manager, Claude Auzello, was waiting and conducted him to the Cambon Bar, from which he did not emerge for several days.

OLIVIER DABESCAT AND MARCEL PROUST

For 60 years the Ritz's *maître d'hôtel*, Olivier Dabescat, ran its restaurant. A lover of titles and moneyed guests, he was famous for telling each guest, 'I have given Monsieur the best table'. Dabescat welcomed two Princes of Wales to the Ritz as well as numerous Russian Grand Dukes. He also sourced live rabbits for the Marchesa Casati's boa constrictor and live pigeons for the hooded falcon of Mrs McLean of the USA. On Christmas Day 1900 he responded to a request from an American guest who wanted to eat an elephant's foot by purchasing an elephant from the zoo and having it killed and served.

Dabescat's friendship with the eccentric Marcel Proust was well known and the author almost definitely immortalised him as Aimé at the Grand Hôtel de Balbec in *À la recherche du temps perdu*. In July 1917 Proust was dining at the Ritz with Jean Cocteau when Gotha heavy bombers of the Imperial German Air Service began attacking Paris. As the air raid siren on the Eiffel Tower went off, Cocteau remarked, 'Someone's trodden on the Eiffel Tower's toe'.

During the war Olivier Dabescat tried to get round the ban on Allied officers drinking alcohol when on leave by serving whisky and champagne in teapots. When arrested by the gendarmes he appealed to a long-term resident who was also a friend of former Prime Minister Clemenceau. The charges were dropped.

Marie-Louise Ritz died in 1961. Up until her last days she still inspected every floor of the hotel. Her son Charles, who had been drafted into the family business in 1927, continued running the hotel until his own death in 1976 when his daughter, César Ritz's granddaughter Monique, took over. By this time the hotel needed a lot of money if it was to keep up with a new generation of luxury hotels. This came in the form of Egyptian businessman Mohamed Al-Fayed who bought the Ritz in 1979.

It was through the Al-Fayed connection that Diana, Princess of Wales left the Ritz early on the morning of 31 August 1997 with her lover Dodi Al-Fayed in a fast car pursued by photographers. The death of Princess Diana, Dodi and driver Henri Paul caused emotional shockwaves around the world, and ensured that the name of the Ritz will now be associated not just with impeccable service and great luxury but with tragic love.

THE CARLTON HOTEL, CANNES (1911)
INTERCONTINENTAL CARLTON CANNES HOTEL

The former British Lord Chancellor Henry, 1st Baron Brougham and Vaux helped established Cannes as a holiday resort after his retirement from politics in 1834. Brougham's villa on the slopes of Croix des Gardes encouraged other British aristocrats to overwinter in France. Later in the century they were joined by wealthy Russians led by Grand Duke Michael Mikhailovich. The Grand Duke, brother of Tsar Alexander III, left Russia in 1891 to live in Cannes with the granddaughter of Alexander Pushkin whom – by the rules of the Romanoff court – he could only marry morganatically. This Russian enclave in Cannes spent lavishly and promoted the sport of sailing along its stretch of coastline.

To cater for this expansion in tourism, new port facilities were built and a boulevard along the shoreline created where once a small beachside oratory had stood. To commemorate its small cross, the boulevard was named Promenade de la Croisette.

Many hotels were constructed, demolished and rebuilt along La Croisette in the nineteenth and early twentieth centuries, but one stood out head, shoulders and cupolas above them all. This was the Carlton, brainchild of the Grand Duke himself and Henry Ruhl, yet another Swiss-born hotelier but one who had taken British citizenship. In the first years of the twentieth century Ruhl had built and bought his way up through a number of French hotels – including the Carlton Champs-Elysées in Paris and the in Carlton at Biarritz. What happened next can be read two ways. In 1907 when the Grand Duke decided that his many sun-seeking guests needed a well-appointed hotel with all modern amenities he looked for a partnership with Ruhl. Or Ruhl, having triumphed in Nice, looked to open a hotel in Cannes and wished the Grand Duke to finance it. Either way the two men agreed that their model was London's new Carlton Hotel which César Ritz had opened in 1902.

Their architect was Charles Dalmas who had already designed a number of Neoclassical hotels along the Côte d'Azur, including two in Nice for Ruhl. Now César Ritz was retired, Auguste Escoffier, his pioneering executive chef, was brought in to design the kitchens.

The new Carlton in Cannes was built in two stages: from 1909 to 1910 the south and east wings were created in time for the opening in 1911; then between 1912 and 1913 a west wing was added, giving the hotel its current U shape.

The floor plan was not the hotel's most distinctive feature, however. Dalmas, working with local architect Marcellin Mayère, envisioned a gigantic white construction facing the sea, decorated with two turrets, one on each corner, both of which would be surmounted by a cupola, the form of which, allegedly, was inspired by the breasts of 'La Belle Otéro'.

The Spanish dancer Carolina Otero was the most famous courtesan of the French Riviera in the years before the First World War, counting Edward Prince of Wales, Grand Duke Nikolay Nikolayevich and Grand Duke Peter Nikolayevich (two cousins of Grand Duke Michael) among her lovers. The Carlton's elegant seventh-floor formal dining room was named La Belle Otéro in her honour (today this entire floor is a series of VIP suites named after movie stars who have triumphed at the Cannes Film Festival like, Grace Kelly, Alain Delon, Sean Connery and Uma Thurman).

In 1917, unsurprisingly, the hotel lost a lot of its Russian clientele following the Bolshevik revolution. It became a hospital in the last months of the First World War. By 1919 business was so bad that the Carlton was sold for one million francs, much less than it had cost to build.

In the 1920s fewer British and German tourists came to Cannes, but the American market opened up, especially at the Carlton which, in 1930, broke with tradition and stayed open during the summer months for the first time.

In January 1922 the British Prime Minister David Lloyd George and his French counterpart Aristide Briand requisitioned the Carlton to accommodate the first Supreme Council of the League of Nations which met to discuss a moratorium on German war reparations. Also present were representatives of Germany, Japan and Italy, as well as an Italian journalist from *Avanti* newspaper who was expelled because he was making too much noise. Benito Mussolini

Photo: Krzysztof Biegański

had the last laugh, however – after the French surrender of 1940, Cannes was occupied by Mussolini's troops.

ROMANTIC RUSSIANS

The last romantic Romanoff at the Carlton was Grand Duke Michael Alexandrovich, fifth child of Emperor Alexander III of Russia and youngest brother of Nicholas II. He was a tragic figure, not only one who defied his family and his Tsar to marry for love, but the first Romanoff to be executed during the Russian Revolution. The object of Michael's affections was Natalia Sergeyevna Wulfert, the wife of a fellow officer and a commoner. Tsar Nicholas, who needed Michael respectably married at court, forbade the marriage. In September 1912, emulating his uncle, Duke Michael fled to Cannes, marrying Natalia en route in Vienna. When the Grand Duke wrote of this to his brother, Nicholas relieved him of his army command, froze all his assets and estates in Russia, and exiled him.

Fortunately the couple had enough money to live on for a while in Cannes. Eventually they moved to a stately home near London until 1914 when Michael was allowed back in to Russia to fight in the First World War. He was captured three years later and shot by the Bolsheviks, aged 39. Natalia, begrudgingly granted the title Countess Brasova by Nicholas, died penniless in a Parisian charity hospital in 1952.

The hotel remained open for business as usual under the Vichy regime and became a popular rendezvous for spies. As in many French hotels, a secret cache was bricked up in the cellar to safeguard the most valuable bottles of wine.

In June 1944 the Vichy authorities closed the Carlton – and the beach was mined – ahead of an expected Allied invasion. But in August American troops landed at Saint-Raphaël, and the 1st French Army landed at Saint-Tropez. The war came to an end quickly for Cannes and its most famous hotel reopened.

Now a film festival that had been under preparation in 1939 was finally launched in 1946 using the Carlton to accommodate its jury. The hotel quickly became the focus of the international festival, because of its location and because so many winners of the Palmes d'Or chose to stay there. The Carlton is now synonymous with the world of movies, so much so that it is one of the few hotels in the world to which Elizabeth Taylor brought all seven of her husbands. It was also here that Faye Dunaway continued the tradition of demanding divas by ordering gallons of goats' milk for her bath.

Movies have also been shot in the hotel, including in 1953 Alfred Hitchcock's *To Catch a Thief*, with Grace Kelly and Cary Grant dining in its Grand Salon and memorably embracing outside bedroom 623. This story of cat-burglars began a tradition that continues today with the InterContinental (since 1982) Carlton being used as a location for heist movies like *French Kiss* (with Meg Ryan and Kevin Kline) and *The Love Punch* (with Emma Thompson and Pierce Brosnan), both of which feature the theft of diamonds at the hotel. Not surprisingly perhaps, the Carlton hotel has also been the scene of some of the most audacious jewellery heists in history, the most recent in 2013.

The hotel remains as glamorous as one of the Romanoffs' Fabergé eggs.

GERMANY

FRANKFURTER HOF, FRANKFURT (1876)
STEINBERGER FRANKFURTER HOF

For a thousand years the free city of Frankfurt was one of the major trading cities of the German-speaking world. In 1871 with the foundation of the German Empire, Prussia as good as annexed Frankfurt, an act which increased the number of visiting businessmen and tourists but was an unpopular move with the city's liberal press. Among those liberal journalists was Leopold Sonnemann, publisher of the *Frankfurter Zeitung,* who had fled the city when Bismarck's troops briefly occupied Frankfurt in 1866 and rounded up the free press.

By 1871 Sonneman was back and involved with a corporation called Frankfurter Hotel Aktiengesellschaft, which wanted to create a new hotel in Frankfurt that was worthy of empire. Berlin was already building its Kaiserhof (*hof* meaning 'court') so this new hotel, initially called Grand Hôtel de Francfort, was also known as the Frankfurter Hof. A site was chosen on Kaiserplatz, named after the new emperor. This would stand at the end of a new Kaiserstrasse linking the brand-new railway station to the old city.

Sonnemann helped raise 3.5 million marks and was instrumental in bringing in architects Mylius and Bluntschli whom he'd met in Vienna. With Sonnemann's encouragement they designed to impress. There would be a great dining room with a domed ceiling supported by 32 marble columns, a winter garden and a cellar large enough to house 20,000 litres of wine in Bordeaux casks. The elevators were constructed in Paris, the marble fireplaces were built in Strasbourg, and the furniture came from Berlin. A startling innovation by the architects was a courtyard cut out of the main façade on Kaiserplatz. While hotel guests would check in at the top of a flight of steps leading from Bethmannstrasse, guests arriving to dine could walk under five noble arches and through the courtyard. On each arch a coat of arms displayed the names of cities alongside which Frankfurt expected to be ranked: Berlin, London, Paris, Rome and St Petersburg.

The hotel opened in June 1876. It was heated by a phenomenal boiler room that also supplied the steam-powered lifts and provided a (not always reliable) supply of electric lighting. There was a post office and a railway desk to help with train reservations for guests as well as shops selling luxury goods like ivory, cigars, and tapestries. Such was the hotel's confidence in its elevators (known as 'rising rooms') that bedrooms on the top floor were not discounted as was normal practice at the time. In its first year the hotel received 38,000 guests and 19,000 diners. Frankfurt's new luxury hotel was so popular that the management declared an open day when citizens queued up to be shown round for an entrance fee of one mark (which was donated to charity).

Internationally the hotel was advertised in the French fashion, and the name Grand Hôtel de Francfort was carved above the five courtyard arches. Just below the roof line, however, its alternative name, Frankfurter Hof, was emblazoned.

Sonnemann's hotel enjoyed a good few years of acclaim. That inveterate traveller and connoisseur of grand hotels,

Mark Twain, stayed in October 1891 and encouraged Americans to visit the city, declaring to his readers that, 'in Frankfurt all the people are neatly dressed. To keep a country as tidy as Germany also has a prudent side to it: it employs and feeds thousands of people that would otherwise be idle and get into mischief.'

Sadly the following year the world's fifth cholera pandemic (1881–96) reached Hamburg. It caused a big drop in the number of American tourists to Germany. A crash on the New York Stock Exchange in 1893 further undermined that burgeoning travel market. Overextended and facing a financial crisis, the executive board of Frankfurter Hotel Aktiengesellschaft made overtures to the one man who they felt could save them – Swiss hotel wizard César Ritz – and offered him the lease.

Ritz, severely overstretched but infinitely ambitious, formed a consortium consisting of himself, Otto Kahn who had bought him Restaurant de la Conversation in Baden-Baden, and Otto's nephews Otto and Ferdinand Hillengass. Georges Gottlob, who had worked for Ritz at London's Savoy, was brought in to run the hotel, and Escoffier, the King of Chefs, helped design the kitchens and the menu. In 1902 Ritz, aware of the allure of his own name, converted the Ladies' Salon into the new Ritz Restaurant (now the Restaurant Français).

During the First World War the hotel donated an annex to serve as a hospital, but continued to offer the best hospitality it could to paying guests despite chronic food shortages. At the very end of the War to End All Wars, the Frankfurter Hof played a dramatic part. On 9 November 1918, two days before the Armistice, an insurrection by German sailors in Kiel spread throughout Germany. In Frankfurt the executive committee of the Soldiers' Council seized the hotel to serve as its headquarters. They set up machine guns under the five famous archways and raided the wine cellar.

RITZ AND THE FUTURE EDWARD VII

When he failed to persuade his most influential patron, Britain's Prince of Wales, to visit the Frankfurter Hof, César Ritz did something typically extravagant. In 1895 while the Prince was staying at Bad Homburg, the hotel was catering a reception at Burgschwalbach 55 kilometres away from the royal personage. Ritz, in London, was determined to bring the Prince along, so he travelled to Germany to persuade him in person. Having succeeded he then hired a railway carriage to transport not just food and wine but the contents of the Frankfurter Hof's kitchens to impress the Prince. Much to Ritz's delight, the ensuing reports of the banquet in the London press especially commended the catering. The Frankfurter Hof was suddenly a destination hotel for wealthy British travellers.

The history of Germany after the First World War – the runaway inflation and the rise of the Nazi party – is all too familiar. Glamour returned to the hotel but many feared a second world war was imminent. It wasn't until 1941 that the first RAF bombing raids on Frankfurt took place. The hotel survived despite its proximity to the strategically important Hauptbahnhof. Then in March 1944 a number of heavy raids targeted the city. On the night of 22 March nearly 1,000 British bombers hit the old town, destroying its medieval core and 83 per cent of the Frankfurter Hof. Albert Steinberger, a hotelier from Baden-Baden who had bought the hotel in 1939, was on the site immediately, overseeing what could be salvaged. He was unimpressed when a Nazi SA (Assault Division) assembled in Kaiserplatz playing military music and declaring proudly, 'Frankfurt is now a frontline city!'

One terrible year later in March 1945, after much street fighting, the American 5th Infantry Division drove the remnants of the German 80th Korps from Frankfurt. The hotel (and indeed the city) was fortunate to end up in the American sector, unlike the Adlon Hotel in Berlin which fell to the Russians.

Soon Albert Steinberger was able to present a report to the US Military Commissioner detailing how much it would cost (6,540,000 marks) and how long it would take (three years) to rebuild the hotel. He was referred to the local reconstruction authority who told him that the Frankfurter Hof should be demolished and reconstructed in a modern style (the plan for the rest of the area around Kaiserplatz). Steinberger stubbornly refused, explaining – brilliantly if untruthfully – that the building was listed and couldn't be demolished. As all the city's records had been destroyed in the bombing, the reconstruction authority conceded. The hotel was rebuilt as it had been, which is why today it is the only vestige of Imperial Germany in this modern section of Frankfurt.

THE ADLON HOTEL, BERLIN (1907)
HOTEL ADLON KEMPINSKI

The Adlon Hotel has had a dramatic life – in fact and in fiction. In the film *Cabaret* Sally Bowles visited it in search of her father, and it was blown up – despite Liam Neeson's best endeavours – in the film *Unknown*.

The hotel, which became a much-loved Berlin institution in the early years of the twentieth century, began its life in controversy. A Neo-Renaissance palace had stood opposite the Brandenburg Gate since 1830. By 1900 it was in need of major restoration which the debt-ridden Grafen von Redern could not afford. In 1905 Lorenz Adlon, a wine merchant and restaurateur from Mainz, wanted to buy and demolish the palace and build the kind of modern international luxury hotel found in London, Paris and New York. Berliners opposed the idea, but Kaiser Wilhelm II, who wished to see the entire Pariser Platz area in front of the Gate redesigned, waived listed building status.

Despite continued attempts to sabotage his plan, Adlon opened the hotel in 1907. Behind an austere façade and under a huge roof it offered 305 bedrooms and 140 bathrooms, which was considered luxurious by German standards of the time.

The strict regime of its hardworking owner and a lot of modern innovations made the Adlon popular. These innovations included an on-site laundry in the attic and its own power plant to ensure a constant supply of electricity. It also had very large public areas and lobbies, a palm court and an interior garden – with an oriental-looking elephant fountain – as well as many ballrooms, making it an ideal place for Berlin society to meet. Despite its restrained modern exterior, the public rooms were decorated in a historic mix of Baroque and Louis XVI styles. The Kaisersaal had a large carved fireplace with a bust of the young Kaiser Wilhelm II over it. A reproduction of this fireplace can be seen in the modern Adlon's Kaisersaal dining room today. Furnishings were by Bembé of Mainz, where Lorenz Adlon had been an apprentice carpenter in his youth.

The new hotel occupied an ideal position to accommodate visiting royalty and heads of state. It was next to the British Embassy and faced the French and American Embassies on Pariser Platz. It was only a few blocks from the Reich Chancellery and other government ministries further south on Wilhelmstrasse.

As the rooms in the Hohenzollern royal palace were cold and draughty, the Kaiser paid an annual retainer to keep suites at the Adlon available for his guests. Visitors before the First World War included Thomas Edison, Henry Ford, and John D. Rockefeller (who was observed sitting with his entourage at breakfast being told not to order any more toast by his doctor). Tsar Nicholas II of Russia came to stay, as did the hugely wealthy Maharaja Bhupinder Singh of Patiala, the first Indian to own an aeroplane. Not surprisingly the hotel's ballrooms were used for official government functions in preference to rooms at the deeply uncomfortable Stadtschloss.

After the First World War and the difficult Weimar years, Lorenz's son Louis Adlon made the hotel one of the most famous in Europe. All the travelling celebrities – Louise Brooks, Charlie Chaplin, Albert Einstein, Enrico Caruso plus Josephine Baker and Marlene of course – stayed at the Adlon, as did Thomas Mann in 1919 on his way to Stockholm to collect the Nobel Prize for Literature.

Under Louis the hotel's lobby was famous for its silence, a quality insisted upon by the Generaldirektor whom the staff referred to simply as 'The Patron'. Louis lived as well as many of his customers. When he attended the theatre, his chauffeur would get out and roll the Adlon red carpet to the theatre door.

Yet there was also a racier side to the Adlon. It held regular tea dances where Berlin's surplus of single women – many of them quite wealthy – could be squired by an *Eintänzer* (taxi dancer) – a man paid to dance and generally make himself agreeable. Because the ladies could not make the first move, hotel pages were given generous tips if they informed one of these handsome young bucks whom they should invite to dance. The men, sometimes described euphemistically as 'failed officers', could make a good living this way.

FATHER AND SON

After the First World War and the abdication of the Kaiser, Lorenz Adlon remained a staunch monarchist. He never came to terms with the fact that normal traffic could now pass through the Brandenburg Gate's central archway, which had hitherto been reserved for the Kaiser alone. He therefore pointedly refused to look for vehicles before crossing in front of it. This resulted in Adlon being hit by a car in 1918 in front of the gate. Three years later, he was again hit by a car at exactly the same spot and died a few days later on 7 April 1921.

Lorenz's son Louis ran the Adlon until the end of the Second World War when he was arrested at his home near Potsdam. It seems that Soviet troops mistook the distinguished-looking hotelier for a Wehrmacht general because of his title of 'Generaldirektor'.

He died of a heart attack on 7 May 1945, two days after the Adlon accidentally burned down.

Louis Adlon tried to stay out of politics, but he was obliged to fly Nazi flags on special occasions. With the outbreak of the

Second World War the Adlon retained its wealthy clientele by constructing a luxurious air raid shelter for guests, and its staff were given blanket exemption from military service on the basis that the Reich deemed them *unentbehrliche* (indispensable).

The Nazi hierarchy generally preferred the Hotel Kaiserhof close to Adolf Hitler's Chancellery. This meant that the bar of the Adlon was an easier place for foreign journalists to try and get information, but when the Kaiserhof was severely damaged in an air raid in November 1943 the Adlon inherited Nazi patronage.

As fighting grew dangerously close to Berlin – no city sustained more nights of bombing during the war – the Adlon built a huge brick wall around its ground floor to protect the function rooms from flying debris, and it sealed off its cellar. Parts of the hotel were converted to a military field hospital during the final days of the Battle of Berlin, but the Adlon survived the war without any major damage. It was seized on 2 May by the Red Army, who took a famous picture of the Soviet flag being held on an Adlon balcony with the Brandenburg Gate beyond. Unfortunately that night some soldiers used grenades to blast their way into the wine cellar, got very drunk and set fire to it. By the morning most of the hotel was left in ruins.

Under the Communist East German government the hotel's service wing was reopened as Hotel Adlon but it bore no relation to the original. The shell of the main building was demolished in 1952, along with all of the other buildings on Pariser Platz. All that was left was the Brandenburg Gate sitting alone behind the infamous Berlin Wall.

With the reunification of Germany in 1989, the site was bought by a West German investment firm. A new hotel was built between 1995 and 1997 which looks remarkably like the old Adlon from the outside, despite subtle enlargement. It also created many of the old rooms and reintroduced the idiosyncratic elephant fountain. Now managed by Kempinski, the Adlon is once again fulfilling its role in Berlin society and welcoming celebrity guests from all over the world, including Michael Jackson who in 2002 shocked the world by dangling his baby son from a hotel balcony.

Herr Generaldirektor would not have approved.

AUSTRIA

HOTEL IMPERIAL, VIENNA (1873)

The Hotel Imperial in Vienna owes its existence directly to the Ringstrasse, a series of linked boulevards that follow the line of the old city walls for six kilometres.

In the mid-nineteenth century Europe was busy tearing down its medieval city walls. They hampered expansion and were ineffective against modern artillery. In any case the continent was enjoying a peace dividend that followed Napoleon's defeat in 1815. By 1857 Vienna was one of the last European capitals to retain its medieval defences. The Habsburg emperor Franz Joseph I (reigned 1848–1916) was conservative in all matters to the point of being bone-headedly unimaginative. It was wholly in his nature to put off the decision to demolish anything.

Finally in 1857 Franz Joseph bowed to the wishes of his people with an imperial decree called *Es ist Mein Wille* ('It is my will'). This promulgation ordered the demolition of the walls and moats, and the construction of a great boulevard within the former *glacis* or no man's land. Rather than open up this 'Ring' around the city to speculative building, the Habsburg government stipulated not just the size of the boulevard but exactly what was to be built along it. The Ringstrasse would be a showcase for the grandeur and glory of the Empire. Palaces, museums, concert halls were de rigueur. Hotels and restaurants were not.

The Ring was a success. It not only became one of the main sights of the city in its own right, it created its own architectural style, *Ringstrassenstil*, an eclectic form of historicism that these days provides the backdrop when we imagine the world of Johann Strauss II, Karl Kraus, Mahler, and Klimt. It's no exaggeration to say that nineteenth-century Viennese life, with all its intrigue and hedonism, is a by-product of the Ringstrasse.

The Emperor was keen that aristocrats and even members of the royal family build themselves palaces around the Ring. He didn't want it to be the preserve of the Jewish plutocracy (whose new wealth he nevertheless was happy to tap to finance the constructions). Prince Philip of Württemberg, who was about to be married to the Habsburg Archduchess Maria Theresa, was one of those who commissioned a home. Palais Württemberg occupied a city block on the corner of what are now known as Schubertring and Kärntner Ring. The architects were Zanetti of Munich and Heinrich Adam from Vienna. The building was completed in 1865 and was notable for its large central portal through which carriages would pass to set down the Prince's visitors inside an inner courtyard where a grand staircase led off to the right. (To this day the hotel's main staircase still leads off to the right rather than rising in front of the visitor as it would in a purpose-built hotel.)

Prince Philip was soon dissatisfied with his new home. The creation of Giselastrasse behind the palace and on it the construction of Vienna's new Musikverein concert hall meant that the Württemberg palace was never going to have a garden. Besides, the Prussian prince was an unsuccessful gambler running out of funds and could not afford its upkeep. So in 1872 he sold the palace to Horace Ritter von Landau who wanted to create a truly regal hotel in time for

Photo: Erich Schmid

the World Fair which was due to take place in Vienna in 1873. (World Fairs were responsible for a lot of speculative hotel building in the nineteenth century.)

The conversion involved installing telephones and elevators, glassing in the courtyard where Prince Philip's coachmen would have turned his horse and carriage round, and converting the Prince's own suite on the *piano nobile* into an extensive Royal Suite. Unlike the purpose-built Hotel Hansen that was being created on Schottenring for the same World Fair, this building would have rooms of different sizes that could usefully reflect the status of its guests. Despite the construction of a whole extra floor on the roof, the conversion was completed in less than twelve months, with the newly named Hotel Imperial opening its doors on 28 April 1873, three days before the Emperor opened the World Fair.

FRANCE V. PRUSSIA

Despite a cholera epidemic, the flooding of the Danube and a stock market crash in May 1873, the Vienna Exposition was a great success, especially for the Imperial Hotel. Two heads of state, Emperor Dom Pedro II of Brazil and Christian IX of Denmark, stayed at the Imperial. So did the Chief of State of France, Patrice de MacMahon, and Chancellor Otto von Bismarck of Prussia. As the rival powers – recent combatants in the Franco-Prussian War – both wanted the Royal Suite, Horace Ritter von Landau divided it in two with a room left empty in between. As both halves had bathrooms, all parties were happy.

The Imperial's reputation received a boost when it was leased in 1874 to the celebrated Hungarian hotelier Johann Frohner. He campaigned for years to get 'By Royal Appointment' status from the Emperor. He failed – but along the way he made the Imperial the hotel of choice for many of the biggest names visiting Vienna. Richard Wagner stayed here with his family in seven rooms in 1875 when conducting *Tannhäuser* and *Lohengrin* at the Wienerstaatsoper. He also gave a dinner for 40 distinguished guests at the Imperial – but it's likely someone else paid for it.

In 1892 Sarah Bernhardt stayed at the Imperial while performing in Vienna, and in 1893 King George of Greece stayed here virtually next door to the Khedive of Egypt. The hotel's café – home of the chocolate, almond and marzipan Imperialtorte – attracted a lot of Vienna's café society including Mahler, Bruckner, and Brahms. The writers Rainer Maria Rilke and Karl Kraus were also regulars.

As its fame spread, so the hotel aimed to grow taller, although the First World War, financial insecurity in the 1920s and Austrian bureaucracy meant that plans for two extra floors were approved in 1913 but not actually implemented until 1929.

According to rumour the young Adolf Hitler worked at the Imperial when an art student in Vienna. He certainly stayed at the Imperial later as Führer following the Anschluss that united Austria and Germany in 1938. Benito Mussolini also stayed at the hotel during the Second World War, under a certain amount of duress. After the success of Allied forces in Italy, Il Duce had become the least popular person in his own country and had to be 'rescued' by German paratroopers in Unternehmen Eiche (Operation Oak). Something of a liability for the Führer by September 1943, Mussolini was slipped in through the hotel's back door to avoid recognition.

After the war Vienna was divided between the four Allied powers and the Imperial found itself in the Soviet sector. For some years it was even the KGB headquarters in Vienna. The Soviets took good care of the building, but when they left they removed a lot of guest books and paperwork to Moscow.

In the 1990s the process of restoring the Imperial to something of the grandeur that Prince Philip and his bride had envisaged was begun. A mezzanine was removed from the lobby to restore the original height of its ceilings and 1,000 marble tiles were relaid across its floor. Further restoration continued into the twenty-first century. Today the Imperial once again lives up to its name but until the old KGB achives are opened up we'll remain in the dark about which rooms Hitler, Wagner and Mussolini took.

HOTEL SACHER, VIENNA (1876)
HOTEL SACHER WIEN

Many grand hotels have invented special dishes – the Parker House Roll in Boston and the Savoy's Peach Melba in London – but only one hotel owes much of its a success to a chocolate cake.

In 1876 Eduard Sacher, son of the celebrated tortemeister and purveyor to the Imperial Court, opened a *maison meublée* (small hotel of furnished rooms) on the site of the demolished Theater am Kärntnertor. The theatre, which had seen premieres by Mozart, Salieri and Haydn as well as the Vienna debut of a pianist called Frédéric Chopin, had been demolished in 1870 after Vienna's Staatsoper opened on the Ringstrasse.

ORIGINAL SACHER-TORTE

In 1832 Franz Sacher (1816–1907) was a sixteen-year-old apprentice to Prince Metternich's chef. According to Sacher legend, one night the Prince, Austria's minister of foreign affairs, ordered a special dessert to be created for his VIP guests. 'Let there be no shame on me tonight!' he declared.

Unfortunately on the day in question the chef was taken ill so young Sacher, in his second year of apprenticeship, was deputised and came up with a glazed chocolate cake with jam that made his name overnight.

Eduard Sacher had not set out to be a hotelier. He had worked his way up from an apprenticeship at Vienna's famous Patisserie Demel and in 1873 at the age of 30 had opened his first restaurant on Kärntner Strasse. But now Vienna was enjoying a hotel spree and Eduard chanced his hand. This fledgling hotel occupied a prime position behind the Staatsoper and had the added lure of Franz's original cake recipe, but the enterprise was given a necessary shot in the arm in 1880 when Eduard married the remarkable Anna Fuchs (1859–1930), who became manager after his death in 1892. Anna did not come from a hotel family either. She was the daughter of a Viennese butcher but she had her eyes firmly on an aristocratic clientele. Frau Sacher quickly earned a reputation for both her commercial skills and her idiosyncratic style, never seen out in Vienna without her French bulldogs or a cigar between her teeth.

Under Anna's strict rule, Hotel Sacher became a very exclusive hotel where the aristocracy and diplomats met.

Emperor Franz Joseph and Empress Sissi visited before the First World War, and Edward and Mrs Simpson afterwards.

The defeat of Austria and the fall of the monarchy in 1918 created chaos in Vienna and changed everything for Hotel Sacher. Austria's new Social Democratic government tried to stem hyperinflation, deal with food shortages and curb various epidemics. Amid the turbulence of 'Red Vienna' Anna Sacher tried to uphold the elite reputation of her hotel in a way that was just not cost-effective. She turned away non-titled guests while at the same time granting very generous credit to impoverished aristocrats. Her management ran Hotel Sacher into financial problems and eventually to bankruptcy.

Nevertheless Frau Anna, like Hotel Sacher, remained a respected Viennese institution. In 1930 after she died in her room at the hotel, tens of thousands lined the streets to the Augustinerkirche to pay their respects as her coffin passed. They were also mourning the passing of the old order.

In 1934 Hans and Poldi Gürtler and their friends Josef and Anna Siller bought the hotel under the company name 'Eduard Sacher GmbH & Co OHG'. The new company brought in sufficient finances to restore the building to its pre-war glory days. Unfortunately in 1938 Anschluss Österreichs (a peaceful unification with Nazi Germany) dealt a blow to tourism, exacerbated – to say the least – by the outbreak of the Second World War eighteen months later.

In the closing months of the Second World War Vienna was badly bombed and 20 per cent of the city obliterated. Although the back of the Staatsoper was destroyed by American incendiaries, Hotel Sacher, only a few metres away, was hardly damaged. The hotel fell first into Russian hands, then became part of the British zone as Vienna was divided and the Russian occupying authorities moved their offices down Kärntner Ring to the Imperial Hotel.

During the ten-year occupation, the British commandeered the hotel as their headquarters. It also provided a room in 1948 to Graham Greene who arrived in Vienna to research Carol Reed's film *The Third Man*. Greene developed the film's idea during conversations in the Sacher bar where he was introduced to Peter Smolka, East European correspondent of *The Times*. It was Smolka who came up with the film's black-market backstory. When the movie was shot the following year, most of the cast and Graham Greene himself stayed at the Sacher, but Orson Welles, who had a turbulent relationship with the film – as with most things – chose to stay further along Kärntner Strasse at the Astoria.

These were not easy times in Vienna, as *The Third Man* accurately portrays. In August 1947, two suitcase bombs had exploded in the basement of Hotel Sacher. The Zionist terrorist group Irgun claimed responsibility.

It wasn't until 1951 that 'Eduard Sacher GmbH & Co OHG' took back control of their hotel from the British. In the years that followed, the hotel expanded around several small courtyards nearby to the rear of the building, and new banqueting rooms were created.

In 1962 after the deaths of Anna and Josef Siller the hotel became the sole property of the Gürtler family, which it still is today. High-profile guests during the 1960s ranged from President Kennedy to John Lennon and Yoko Ono, who in March 1969 gave a 'Bagism' press conference in Hotel Sacher. Bagism involved literally wearing a bag over one's body to avoid being judged by any visual attributes. As ever in Vienna, the idea was politely received.

In 1970 Hans Gürtler's son Rolf took over running the now legendary hotel but died soon after, leaving his son Peter in charge at the young age of 25. Peter Gürtler expanded the Sacher enterprise, taking over the Österreichischer Hof hotel in Salzburg, which was renamed the Hotel Sacher Salzburg in 2000, and opening the first Sacher Cafés: Innsbruck in 1999 and Graz in 2003.

The hotel is now run by the Peter's wife, Elisabeth Gürtler-Mauthner, and Original Sacher Torte is still served in the hotel's restaurants and café. About 360,000 hand-made cakes are shipped all over the world each year.

Truly this was a hotel that was built from a cake.

SWITZERLAND

HÔTEL DES BERGUES, GENEVA (1834)
FOUR SEASONS HÔTEL DES BERGUES

Switzerland's first purpose-built hotel was constructed on an uninspiring shore of Lake Geneva. In 1816 when Lord Byron, Percy Bysshe Shelley, and Mary Wollstonecraft Godwin travelled to Switzerland – and scared themselves silly during a thunderstorm at Villa Diodati – they avoided the city entirely, which included the foul-smelling quayside known as Bergues.

At the beginning of the nineteenth century Bergues was a manufacturing suburb of Geneva, specialising in watch-making and textile-printing. It stood on the north bank of the River Rhône as it flowed out of Lake Geneva. Bergues was an industrial slum of depressing meanness. While it was possible to find an inn here, the English party were put off by the food riots of 1816. The long-term devastation of Napoleon's wars and the worst summer on record had resulted in food shortages across Europe and many European cities were in turmoil. No wonder Mary Shelley's novel *Frankenstein* was born in a villa at a safe distance from Geneva itself.

A few years later, however, Bergues's prospects began to look up. In 1823 the first tourist steamboat arrived on the lake and changed Geneva's attitude to its malodorous quayside. Businessmen and burghers alike recognised that this waterfront needed to become more welcoming to visitors.

In 1829, the Société des Bergues was formed. This consortium wanted to create a more appealing neighbourhood outside the old city with Switzerland's first grand urban hotel at its centre. They bought the old Jean-Louis Fazy fabric factory on the quayside and demolished it. An architectural competition was held for a hotel that would be 'simple, of pure style and free of superfluous ornamentation'. The winning architect was August Miciol of Lyon. His design, however, was subsequently modified by local architect Samuel Vaucher to create a more impressive building in a plain Neoclassical style. Geneva (recently admitted to the Swiss Confederation) was keen to promote its associations with the republics of ancient Greece and therefore very partial to pediments supported by columns and pilasters.

This new hotel would be linked to the south bank of the Rhône – and thereby to the medieval city of Geneva – by a bridge. The bridge was designed by Colonel Guillaume-Henri Dufour, an engineer who would go on to lead the Swiss Federal Army to victory in 1847 when its Catholic cantons tried to set up their own federation. Dufour's Pont des Bergues crossed the Rhône in two stages a few metres downriver from the entrance to the hotel. The central section of the bridge formed an artillery platform in the middle of the Rhône for defence and was later renamed Île Rousseau.

Dufour was originally only intended to work on the bridges but he also took on a lot of the hotel design, travelling to Paris to see how the Meurices, father and son, were making a success of their new grand hotel. He came back with ideas for elegant public rooms, a ladies' salon, rooms for gaming and a *salon fumoir* for smoking.

Opened on 1 May 1834, Bergues was the largest urban hotel in Switzerland at the time. The ground floor of the hotel was occupied by a café, some shops and a carriage entrance between columns – very like the Meurice's. From street level, stone steps rose up to its *bel étage* (first floor) which offered a modest reception area. Above this mezzanine were three floors of bedrooms with an attic to accommodate staff. Until the introduction of elevators, the higher up your room was, the less you were charged.

The board appointed Alexandre Emmanuel Rufenacht as director. He was a 40-year-old former army captain with the Swiss Regiment that had marched into Russia under Napoleon. His precise, military approach to hotel management quickly established high standards. Nineteenth-century Europe was about to discover the wonder of the Swiss hotelier.

The new Hôtel des Bergues served a double function in Geneva. It was not only there to provide an attractive welcome to tourists, but was also a residence for visiting VIPs. The fortified Calvinist city on the south side of the Rhône had no palaces where royalty or aristocracy could be entertained, so Bergues was always intended as more than a superior coaching inn.

One quirk about the hotel's design today is that its main staircase is a stone spiral leading up from behind the ground floor reception area. Unlike most nineteenth-century hotels, this staircase is neither broad nor central. If it had been, the wind from Lake Geneva would have blown straight up from the open carriage entrance into the hotel proper.

The hotel on the Bergues quayside enjoyed a long and uneventful history, making a lot of money and changing owners occasionally. In 1876 the British physician Francis Sibson, who gave his name to the suprapleural membrane, 'Sibson's fascia', died unexpectedly while on holiday in the hotel but that's about as much drama as Bergues saw in the nineteenth century.

Most news was good news. In 1858 when the railways arrived in Geneva, Bergues received a boost as Cornavin station was only 700 metres up the hill behind the hotel. The best address in Geneva was now the most convenient too.

BUT WHO WAS 'BERGUES'?

The name 'des Bergues' has the kind of pedigree that no hotel would willingly give up. It originated with a German merchant and financier called Johannes Kleberger (1486–1546). Though frequently on his travels, Herr Kleberger owned several properties in Geneva, including one on the section of quayside now known as Bergues. A friend of the theologian Erasmus of Rotterdam, Johannes Kleberger had his portrait painted by Albrecht Dürer. (It can be seen today in Vienna's Kunsthistorisches Museum.)

Herr Kleberger was renowned for his great generosity, which may be why after his death, his impoverished son had to sell the ground where Hôtel des Bergues stands today to cover the family's debts. The site was bought by the City of Geneva and its buildings demolished to create factories, but already locals had begun calling this section of quay on the north bank of the Rhône 'En Clébergue', a name that was eventually became to 'Quai des Bergues' as more and more industry grew up around it.

Between 1917 and 1920, the most recent owners, Société nouvelle des Bergues, undertook a major reconstruction of the hotel, under the Geneva architect Maurice Turrettini.

He remodelled the interior, bringing reception down to the ground floor and introducing seven ionic columns to the façade to make it grander. Reopened in February 1920, the hotel hosted early meetings of the ill-fated League of Nations in its new function room (now called the Salle des Nations).

Bergues became part of the Four Seasons portfolio in 2004. Such was the importance attached to its name by then that Hôtel des Bergues is one of the few Four Seasons properties to have retained its original title. From being a scruffy, polluted nineteenth-century embarrassment where the Shelleys wouldn't stay, the name Bergues has become a status symbol.

BAUR AU LAC, ZURICH (1844)

It's rare for a grand hotel to remain in the hands of the same family for over 150 years but the Baur on Lake Zurich has indeed been run by Johannes Baur's descendants since it was opened in 1844.

The hotel was a daring project by Baur, a baker from Austria who in 1838 had made enough money to open a hotel – Baur en Ville – in the centre of Zurich. With new steamships bringing tourists along Switzerland's lakes, Baur believed that the Zurichsee might become as much of a tourist attraction as the famous city. So in 1842 he bought some land either side of Schanzengraben, the old city moat that ran down to the lake. The only building nearby was the Bauschänzli, an old artificial gun platform island in the River Limmat. Apart from this last vestige of the city's baroque fortifications, there was very little out at the point where lake and river joined.

Baur was a visionary, however. Within a few years the city followed his lead and extended in the direction of the new Baur au Lac. Building the four-storey hotel, essentially a large, square Italianate villa, cost far more than expected. Some of the hotel's land on the other side of the moat was sold off to a wealthy silk manufacturer from Basle who built himself a home there known as Villa Rosau. (The family eventually bought the villa in 1925 and turned it into the renowned Club Baur). As with so many great hotels, early success was down to one obsessive hotelier. Johannes Baur wanted such high standards he micromanaged everything, running a white-gloved finger along the furniture each day to check for dust.

Maybe it was the remote, romantic lakeside location, but from its beginning the Baur au Lac drew guests who were travelling incognito. King Oscar of Sweden stayed under the name the Comte de Tulgran. Ulysses S. Grant and the Duchesse d'Orléans also stayed anonymously (but separately). In fact a *nom d'aventure* was such a regular occurrence that the Baurs claim that when the Habsburg Empress Sissi visited in 1867 she was their first European celebrity to have the bills made out in her own name.

In 1852 Baur, now aged 57, handed the running of the hotel over to his son Theodor, who the following year had the interesting experience of hosting Richard Wagner. As well as attracting aristocrats and royalty, the romantic hotel by the lake also appealed to artists – if they could afford it. Or in Richard Wagner's case if someone else could afford it for him. The diminutive musical genius and irrepressible egoist was in Zurich as a guest of local silk merchant Otto Wesendonck, for whom he performed the entire libretto of his (as yet uncomposed) *Der Ring des Nibelungen* at the hotel. Standing in the drawing room, known as the Petit Palais, Wagner spoke, sang, muttered and shouted the lengthy poem over four nights. Each evening more and more people stopped by for this unconventional free show. After the last instalment, the wealthy Wesendonck presented Wagner with a substantial cheque to finance his Ring Cycle project. Wagner reciprocated by making a pass at Wesendonck's wife, Mathilde. She in turn responded by falling deeply in love with him.

In 1856 the composer Franz Liszt arrived in Zurich and Wagner – now living in a house lent to him by the Wesendoncks – presented his fellow composer with an unusual birthday present at the Baur. With Liszt sitting – unrehearsed – at the piano, Wagner sang his way through the first act of *Die Walküre*. The evening was a delight for his supporters if mystifying for those who had not yet embraced Wagner's vision for the 'Music of the Future'. For Theodor Baur the performance was particularly satisfying because he harboured hopes of Zurich becoming once again 'the Athens on the Limmat', a city that was the natural home of great artists, as it had been before the Napoleonic Wars.

The following year, Liszt's daughter Cosima visited Wagner in Zurich while on her honeymoon and she also fell in love with him. Eventually this unconventional couple lived together from 1863 in Zurich, much to her indulgent husband's bemusement.

After having Richard Wagner as a guest, everyday hotel life can seem a bit tame. Nevertheless Baur au Lac witnessed some significant moments in nineteenth-century history such as the Treaty of Zurich, which was negotiated in the hotel in 1859 and led ultimately to the process of Italian Unification.

Ludwig I, the deposed king of Bavaria and sometime lover of exotic dancer Lola Montez, came to stay in 1860 and found a soulmate in Theodor Baur. Both were frustrated town-planners and greatly enjoyed discussing architecture together.

The widowed King Leopold I of the Belgians stayed here

Photo: © Kate Tadman-Mourby

in 1863, dining alone in his room, and it would be fair to say that there was rarely a time when one member or other of the Romanoff family was not passing through. In 1892 Alfred Nobel's former secretary, Baroness Bertha von Suttner, convinced the Swedish industrialist that he needed to fund an international peace prize as they sat together under the great circular glass ceiling of the hotel's hall.

After constant enlargements, the hotel reached its present size in 1898, constructed around not one but two courtyards and occupying an entire city block. Following the death of Theodor it was taken over by his son-in-law, Karl Kracht. In June 1902 Kracht witnessed the Great Paris–Vienna Race that passed through Zurich and calculated that the motor car could make the journey to Vienna in less time than a train. Realising that cars were the coming thing, Kracht not only purchased one for himself, he opened Switzerland's first hotel garage on the other side of the Schanzengraben, with its own team of mechanics. The garage – with its petrol pump – still stands there today and has retained its expertise for maintaining vintage cars.

Unusually for a modern hotel the Baur still maintains not just a carpenter and florist on site but a tapestry-maker too. The recent refurbishment of the red leather handrail on the main staircase was completed entirely in-house.

Because Switzerland sat out two world wars, the twentieth century proved less traumatic for the Baur au Lac than for many European hotels. Its roster of heads of state, royalty and celebrities has continued almost unchecked and the hotel has remained a paragon of discretion. In 2015 when seven FIFA executives were taken from their beds at the Baur and bundled into unmarked cars by an American FBI team, the hotel refused to comment. Those involved in what became known as the 'World Cup of Fraud' were shielded from cameras by hotel linen draped over their heads. A spokesman later commented: 'Discretion is one of the hallmarks of the Baur au Lac. Therefore, it is our consistent policy not to make any statements in regards to our esteemed guests. We are sure you will respect our position.'

If Wagner and the Kaiser (see below) couldn't discomfit the Baur, the Feds certainly wouldn't.

THE KAISER

Wilhelm II, the German Kaiser, knew he was not welcome in the French and Italian cantons of Switzerland but in 1912 he insisted on a state visit to a German-speaking Swiss city. He was invited to Zurich and the city proposed he stay at its most famous hotel. The Kaiser proved a difficult guest, refusing to sleep at the Baur where the President of the Swiss Confederation was awaiting him. So it was arranged that the Emperor would sleep on what he regarded as German territory, the nearby former villa of Otto and Mathilde Wesendonck. The Wesendoncks – still married despite her lengthy flirtation with Wagner – had fled their Zurich home in 1871 during anti-German riots.

The Kaiser did agree to dine with President Forrer in the Baur's Petit Palais. He insisted the meal take only one hour and ten minutes. This was the time he always allowed for meals. The hotel still owns the 23-metre-diameter round table at which all 36 guests briefly sat. It is kept in the basement where the hotel's workshops still function today.

GSTAAD PALACE, GSTAAD (1913)

Today the name Gstaad conjures up images of extreme
affluence and famous tanned faces from what used to be
known as the jet-set. At the end of the nineteenth century,
however, the village of Gstaad was in a very sorry state
indeed. In 1898 almost half of it had been destroyed by fire
and new sources of income were desperately needed for
the 150 impoverished inhabitants. The growing fashion for
skiing seemed to offer an answer as Gstaad's high altitude
certainly guaranteed lots of snow. There was a problem,
however. The rail connection from Montreux had been
routed from Saanen to bypass Gstaad. It took six years of
lobbying to get a railway to loop up to Gstaad.

In the early years of the twentieth century one the most
tireless promoters of the village was a young schoolmaster
called Robert Steffen who wrote pamphlets on the beneficial
effects of Gstaad's climate and published the first picture
postcards of the village. He also found investors in Lausanne
and in Geneva for a grand project called the 'Royal-Hôtel
and Winter Palace'. This eventually opened in December
1913. Locals were worried about what looked like a skyscraper
being built on a hill above their village, but its crenellations
gave it a retro-fortified look that calmed concerns of
Manhattan marching into Gstaad.

The hotel had no time to establish itself before the First
World War broke out, but its finances survived. Steffen did
not. He died, worn out at the age of 45, in 1923.

During the 1930s the Palace did well enough in uncertain
financial times, but its real fortune was still to be made by
a man called Ernst Scherz. Scherz had worked in the Swiss

watch-making industry but had always felt the call of hotel life. He followed this strange compulsion first as a waiter at the Hotel Bellevue Palace in Bern, then at the Carlton in London before moving to Shepheard's Hotel in Cairo as a manager.

Back in Switzerland, Ernst Scherz made his way through the top Swiss hotels, eventually – at the young age of 26 – managing the Carlton St Moritz in 1936 with his new wife Sylvia. In 1937, taking a gamble that he was to repeat at the Gstaad Palace, Scherz organised a grand gala concert in the ballroom of the Carlton, for which he hired the renowned opera diva Toti Del Monte. Her fee was a massive 8,000 Swiss francs. The sell-out concert drew an international audience and was a roaring success, generating a lot of column inches. The ticket price of 120 francs, including gala dinner, only just covered the costs, but during the first three months of 1938 there wasn't a single empty bed in the Carlton.

Later that same year Scherz took over from the retiring manager of the Gstaad Palace, as it was now known, but strictly on the basis that he would receive his salary only if the hotel made a profit. By 1942 Scherz had been invited to become majority owner, not something he could afford, nor something he could resist. He took out 25 unsecured loans totalling almost half a million Swiss francs for a hotel that was barely making a profit, and did not sleep well at night.

The Palace did well once peace returned to Europe, however. The Scherz blend of modesty and great competence appealed to the clientele. Royals in particular liked to stay in Gstaad. At one point the entire Spanish royal family and the King of Afghanistan were neighbours at the Gstaad Palace. When King Leopold III of the Belgians announced his arrival, Ernst and Silvia Scherz moved out of their chalet to give the royals their beds.

Hotel life in the late 1940s was different in many ways

from today. The post of *maître de plaisir*, for example, has now ceased to exist but at the Palace for many years this position was filled by the accomplished Fred Deroy, who during the day acted as children's swimming instructor and in the evenings would dance with the ladies whose husbands preferred to stand at the bar.

A DEFECTOR AT THE PALACE

In 1949 the top Czech athlete Jaroslav Drobný defected from Czechoslovakia while playing at a tennis tournament in Gstaad. An international incident ensued and Swiss police were obliged to hunt for Drobný who was hiding in the hotel's cellars. A few weeks later when the clamour died down, Drobný repaid his gratitude towards the people of Gstaad by working as trainer for the Gstaad hockey club before finally finding a country – Egypt – that would give him a passport. He is still the only Egyptian to have won the Wimbledon men's singles title, which he did in 1954.

Ernst Scherz always pursued cultural activities at the hotel, which helped to extend the Palace's renown. In 1956 he set up the Menuhin Festival which, with input from Benjamin Britten and Sir Yehudi Menuhin himself, used churches in the Saanen area as venues. The success of what soon became a major international music festival later inspired Ernst's grandson Thierry to set up a complementary winter festival, Sommets Musicaux, in churches near the Palace, which continues today.

Scherz had always seen the advantages of bringing celebrity entertainers to the hotel as well, especially when combining their performances with gala dinners. The first star he signed up was Maurice Chevalier, who was paid 6,000 Swiss francs for the evening. (Silvia asked her husband whether he was aware of all the things that could be done with that sum at a time when they barely had enough money to replace lightbulbs.) Chevalier came, was a big hit, and used his contacts to encourage other international celebrities to perform in Gstaad. In the 1950s, big stars could only be seen live in Paris, in London, or on Broadway, but Ernst Scherz was determined to add the Palace Hotel in Gstaad to that list. Soon fees of 10,000 Swiss francs were being handed over, astronomic sums in the 1950s. Marlene Dietrich performed with a twenty-piece orchestra from Radio Suisse Romande. Ella Fitzgerald flew in from America. When Maurice Chevalier heard that she was booked, he cancelled several engagements to meet her and the two got on famously, remaining friends for life. It was Louis Armstrong's appearance at the Palace, though, that caused Silvia Scherz to exclaim, 'Now you really have gone crazy!' when she discovered the fee of 40,000 Swiss francs. Gratifyingly the audience included several minor royals.

Thereafter big names became Gstaad's unique selling point, although the family itself continued to live modestly nearby. Still, for Ernst's grandsons having James Bond star Roger Moore come and play with your model train track, or participating in a game of hide-and-seek with French President Jacques Chirac must have given them an unusual view of home life. Young Thierry once sneezed into Liz Taylor's fur stole because she hugged him so tightly its fine hairs tickled his nose.

When you've been hugged by Elizabeth Taylor, the sky really is the limit. That seems to have remained the maxim by which Thierry's brother Andrea runs it today.

ITALY

HÔTEL DE RUSSIE, ROME (1820)

Between 1811 and 1822 the area round Porta Flaminia was transformed under the urban planner and Neoclassical architect Giuseppe Valadier. First he built Piazza del Popolo, one of the most beautiful squares in Rome today. In doing this Valadier demolished a lot of secular buildings to give greater prominence to two seventeenth-century churches that faced the piazza.

Next to the more easterly of the two, Santa Maria in Montesanto, just where the Piazza meets Via del Babuino, he built a palazzo that soon after became the city's most splendid hotel to date. L'Hôtel des Îles Britanniques was constructed in 1816–18 as Palazzo Lucernari. When the British painter J.M.W. Turner sketched the work in progress in 1819, Valadier had not yet converted the palazzo into a hotel but he did so soon after, at the behest of Count Torlonia.

The Torlonias were bankers and Count Giovanni Torlonia was an administrator of the Vatican finances. He provided the capital for this corner of Piazza del Popolo and for the new palace/hotel. The Land Register of 1818 described it 'a large four-storey building with a front façade of two levels of half columns and relief pilasters'. The four pilasters are still on the façade today, although between 1870 and 1871 two further floors were added above the cornice by the architect Nicola Carnevali. A garden was created behind the palazzo which climbed the Pincian Hill in terraces. This hillside had originally been a vineyard and here Valadier, the arch-Neoclassicist, created a waterfall running between three nymphaeums. An English guide published in 1833 referred to Hôtel des Îles Britanniques as 'an excellent Inn which furnishes an hundred and fifty beds'. Given that its top two floors would not be built for another 40 years, Valadier's conversion must have crammed lots of little bedrooms into the palazzo. Even today there are only 121 rooms.

VIA DEL BABUINO

In the sixteenth century three new roads were constructed from Porta Flaminia, the north gate of Rome's city walls, into the centre. One of these was called Via Clementina, in honour of Pope Clement. It was to become one of the routes that pilgrims took into the Spanish Quarter, where foreigners could find lodgings. In 1571, on the initiative of Pope Pius V, a new fountain for public use was installed on the street, and a statue of Silenus, the satyr and companion to Dionysus, was placed nearby. So ugly was the statue that it was compared to a baboon, and the street soon became known Via del Babuino.

We don't know what caused Count Torlonia to redevelop his brand-new palazzo into a hotel, but we do know that the Torlonias were not short of palaces around Rome and that Rome continued to be short of hotels. In 1845 Count Giovanni opened up the old auberge opposite his home, Palazzo Núñez-Torlonia, as another hotel aimed at the

HÔTEL DE RUSSIE, ROME

English traveller. It was named Albergo d'Inghilterra (now Hotel Inghilterra). Both hotels eventually came under the management of hotelier Francesco Nistelweck, who in 1889 would open his own hotel, the Eden (see page 176), at the top of the Spanish Steps. The second half of the nineteenth century was a time of rapid expansion in Roman hoteliery.

In 1853 Charles Dickens stayed at L'Hôtel des Îles Britanniques, arriving on 13 November and departing on the 18th for Florence, a coach journey that took three and a half days (it now takes three hours by car). On 2 November 1862 the novelist Wilkie Collins – never in the best of health – arrived at the hotel complaining of 'the pains of sciatica in both hams'. He was advised that the weather in Naples would suit his legs better and duly went in search of it, but was back on 4 December, his gout no better.

Towards the end of the nineteenth century, when Italy had its first king, the hotel became known as Albergo dei Rei, but as its popularity was growing among the Russian nobility, it took on the name Hôtel de Russie et des Îles Britanniques. (It was a common custom in the nineteenth century to name your hotel after the clientele you hoped to attract.)

Hôtel de Russie was also attracting the French. On 17 March 1891 Napoleon's nephew, Prince Jérôme Napoleon, also known as 'Plon Plon', died at the hotel. He was the senior member of the Bonaparte family and a plaque fixed to the outside of the hotel today commemorates his stay.

A postcard dated 1901 shows that at the beginning of the twentieth century Hôtel de Russie still stood directly on Piazza del Popolo. That was to soon change when two symmetrical buildings were added on the south-east and south-west corners of the piazza, sadly obscuring the view.

In May 1911 the ballet impresario Diaghilev stayed at what was now firmly called Grand Hôtel de Russie when he brought Ballets Russes from Monte Carlo to perform at Teatro Costanzi (now Teatro dell'Opera). While Diaghilev enjoyed de Russie, the rest of the company were spread around the city in less comfort. Stravinsky, who was struggling to complete *The Firebird* at the time (following a bout of nicotine poisoning), stayed nearby at Albergo d'Italia.

In February 1917 Picasso and Jean Cocteau, collaborators on the ballet *Parade*, stayed in rooms 95 and 96 at Grand Hôtel de Russie. Their bill, which sported British and Russian coats of arms but was made out in French (as was still the fashion across Europe), was probably paid by Diaghilev. Each man took a bath during their stay, the cost for which was 2 lire 50 cents each, the same price as a hot chocolate. Cocteau later wrote that staying at the hotel was 'Paradise on Earth', while Picasso came back to Rome the next year on honeymoon with his first wife, Olga Khokhlova, who had danced at the premiere of *Parade*.

After the Russian Revolution many impoverished aristo-crats came to live in a hotel where they had known happier times. The now not-so-extremely-wealthy Prince and Princess Felix Yussupov, whose son had participated in the murder of Rasputin, lived in reduced circumstances at de Russie until the Prince's death in 1928. Lina Cavalieri, the Italian soprano whose famously perfect face was used as a motif for thousands of items created by Italian designer Piero Fornasetti, was also a regular guest.

During the Second World War the hotel was given a more patriotically Italian name: 'Locanda di Russia'. It was then taken over by Military Information Services. After the war, in a rather sorry state, it was bought by the builder and entrepreneur Romolo Vaselli who had been created a Count by the King in 1941. (Suite Vaselli on the fifth floor honours the work he did to restore the property.) In 1969 after Count

Vaselli's death, Locanda di Russia stopped being a hotel altogether and became offices for RAI, the state broadcaster.

In 1999 the property was bought by Sir Rocco Forte, whose sister and head of design, Olga Polizzi, redesigned the hotel while Antonella Daroda restored Valadier's garden. Suites honouring Picasso and the dancer Nijinsky were added and the bar off 'Jardin de Russie' was named after Igor Stravinsky. It reopened in April 2000 with what may be its final name, Hôtel de Russie.

THE GRITTI PALACE, VENICE (1850 – *or* 1948)

When is a hotel not a hotel? Depending on your definition, the Gritti Palace was Venice's first hotel to open on the Grand Canal in the middle of the nineteenth century – or one of the first after the Second World War.

The building we know as the Gritti dates back to at least 1475 when the Pisani family, one of the wealthiest to have its name inscribed in the *Libro d'Oro*, remodelled an existing palace. In the days when Venice dominated Mediterranean trade, all the city's principal families had their name in that book plus status-symbol palaces on the Grand Canal – and usually a country estate where they could sit out the summer.

The Palazzo Pisani was bought by the white-bearded Doge Andrea Gritti in the sixteenth century and it remained in his family until 1777. After a succession of owners, and even a spell as the official residence of Vatican ambassadors to Venice, Palazzo Pisani-Gritti was divided up with one side coming into the possession of Baroness Wetzlar von Plankstern in the late 1840s.

JOHN RUSKIN

The English art critic John Ruskin and his wife Effie Grey occupied rooms in the palazzo after a few weeks at the Danieli in 1849. It hadn't been easy to find an apartment big enough, as Ruskin insisted on a separate bedroom of his own. The artist spent his time sketching the architecture of Venice for his masterwork *The Stones of Venice* (1851–53) while Effie – with his encouragement – flirted with Austrian officers who were occupying the city. Theirs was a peculiar non-marriage, which Effie later had dissolved on the grounds of non-consummation so she could marry the painter John Everett Millais in 1855.

The status of the Gritti at this time was also anomalous. It was perhaps a *maison meublée*, a place where with a personal introduction gentlemen and their ladies of quality could rent furnished rooms for weeks or months – but not quite a commercial hotel like the Danieli which welcomed all-comers.

Ruskin wrote glowingly of the capitals of the Palazzo Pisani-Gritti's first-floor windows as 'singularly spirited and graceful', but he disliked the upper storeys. He would have been even less happy when a fourth floor was added to the palace in 1895, when it became an annex to the Flangini Fini and Mandolesso Ferro palaces next door. At this time the composite 'Palazzo Ferro-Fini' – as it was known locally – was transformed into the Grand Hotel Venice. That building still sits on the Grand Canal but is now government offices.

After the Second World War the Grand Hotel was in a sorry state, having been occupied first by German and then

Photo: Abxhay

by American troops, so in 1948 the Palazzo Pisani-Gritti reopened as a commercial hotel in its own right. It was run by the CIGA (Compagnia Italiana Grandi Alberghi). This was the moment when the Gritti Palace became what it is today. With the Lido ceding popularity to the main islands, the Gritti very quickly established itself as a major hotel in Venice and all the big 1950s names took suites. Winston Churchill, General de Gaulle, Lauren Bacall and Humphrey Bogart, Charlie Chaplin, Greta Garbo, Igor Stravinsky, Somerset Maugham, Graham Greene, Orson Welles, and Frank Lloyd Wright all stayed at the Gritti. Ernest Hemingway was there with his fourth wife Mary Welch. Here he made a fool of himself by becoming infatuated with a local nineteen-year-old, weaving her into his least successful novel. *Across the River and into the Trees* was a personal fantasia in which Hemingway, disguised as a hard-drinking American colonel, dies, having secured the love of a nineteen-year-old Venetian contessa. Unfortunately rather than keeping it to himself, Hemingway published this fantasy in 1950 and garnered the first bad reviews he'd ever received.

By 1979 the Gritti Palace was proving so popular that it decided to stay open over winter for the first time. Nowadays Venice receives so many tourists that hotels like the Cipriani that close for winter are an anomaly, but this year-long opening period in Venice is still a relatively recent phenomenon.

Damaged like so many hotels by persistent flooding, the Gritti closed for a major restoration in 2011 and managed to reopen fifteen months (and $50 million) later looking reassuringly similar but now stable and floodproof. Every item in the Hemingway Suite (named after rooms he had occupied in 1950) had been labelled and cleaned and replaced in its exact position. The faded glass in the Bar

Longhi was no brighter than before and its three priceless genre scenes by the celebrated eighteenth-century painter Pietro Longhi were fitted back in place. The velvet chairs in the library still look as they did in the days when Churchill nearly set them alight with his cigars, and you would never believe that all the terrazzo Veneziano floor covering on the landings had been taken up and relaid piece by piece by hand. The hotel is very proud that everything is *com'era e dov'era* (as it was, where it was) but now sitting on top of a complex flood prevention reservoir.

But not everything is the same. The recent refurbishment, as with all modern hotel refurbishments, cut down the number of rooms (from 92 to 81) and expanded the bedroom size. More use was also made of the canal views. In 1948 Compagnia Italiana Grandi Alberghi had thought it wise to have the best suites facing away from the pungent Grand Canal. Now canal views are at a premium.

In 2011 designer Chuck Chewning created two new VIP suites in addition to the Hemingway and Maugham suites, one commemorating John Ruskin in rich Victorian-style reds and greens, and another commemorating the art collector Peggy Guggenheim, whose own Palazzo Nonfinito is a near neighbour of the Gritti, but who celebrated her 80th birthday here in 1978.

The style of the Gritti today is as it was in 1948, an old palace with an eclectic collection of antiques – the reception desk not only looks like an altar rail, it was actually taken out of a Venetian church that Napoleon had deconsecrated. And the celebrities continue to pile in, with Woody Allen, Bruce Springsteen, Al Pacino, Mick Jagger, Kate Winslet, and Nicole Kidman taking the place of the Bogarts and Bacalls of the 1950s.

LONDRA PALACE, VENICE (1853)
HOTEL LONDRA PALACE

Today Hotel Londra Palace is one of those hotel puzzles that can be found all over Europe. It changed its name frequently as it enlarged and merged with other buildings, but no one thought to keep a record of where famous guests stayed as the hotel was repeatedly bought and sold. Invariably the owner took the guest book and other pieces of memorabilia away when s/he left. The idea of a hotel being a piece of our heritage whose records must be preserved for posterity is relatively recent.

Much of what we do know about the hotel now called Londra Palace can be worked out from inspecting the façade of the building today. Stand at the Alilaguna San Zaccharia station and is obvious that the Londra Palace consists of three unequal structures that have been merged over time.

It all began in 1853 when a new enterprise, the Hôtel d'Angleterre and Pension, was built on the quayside in front of San Zaccharia church to designs by an architect called Rossini. The success of Giuseppe Dal Niel's new commercial hotel inside the old Palazzo Dandalo had encouraged speculative building nearby. Danieli (as Dal Niel was nicknamed in Venice) had opened the hotel that would bear his name in 1822 on the first floor of the old Palazzo Dandalo. Its rapid commercial success enabled him to buy up the entire building in 1824 and restore it lavishly.

The Hôtel d'Angleterre and Pension took its name from the nineteenth-century vogue across Europe for giving hotels English names like London, Bristol, and Carlton. After the defeat of Napoleon, the British were not only Europe's new superpower, they were also wealthy and tireless travellers. It made economic sense to tout for their custom.

Twelve years later in 1865 Hôtel Beau Rivage was built just a few metres away from the Angleterre by a Venetian engineer called Fuin. This was a taller, grander building using Istrian marble in a Neo-Gothic style and was to be Peter Tchaikovsky's home in Venice from November 1877.

Two life-sized lions used to sit outside the entrance to the Beau Rivage. Tchaikovsky was sufficiently fond of them to contemplate calling his new symphony 'Do Leoni' ('Two Lions', in the Venetian dialect). The highly strung composer wrote enthusiastically of working on his fourth symphony in the hotel and recorded, 'Venice is a marvellous city. Every day I discover something new and fascinating. I believe I have fallen desperately in love with this charming maiden.'

The love affair did not last, however, and when the late December weather on the Riva degli Schiavoni grew cold and damp, Tchaikovsky became gloomy and eventually left without even sketching the final movement of his symphony. It never did bear the name Do Leoni.

In 1900 the two hotels were merged to create the 73-room Hôtel Londres et Beau Rivage. A small extra section of hotel in the Beau Rivage's Neo-Gothic style was inserted to link the two buildings. It is easy today to work out that the older, less flamboyant pension made up the right flank of the hotel and the Beau Rivage the left. Inside the hotel on the first to fifth floors there is a set of small steps two-thirds of the way along each corridor at the point where the lower floor level of the Beau Rivage met the slightly higher floors of the Hôtel d'Angleterre. An artist's impression painted in 1900 shows that the join between the two hotels was supposed to be made invisible by adding more Gothic windows across

Photo: Abchay

the façade. Sadly all those Gothic arches were ripped out in the 1950s when the hotel was given a consistent roofline. It is possible, however, to sit in Room 106 (which honours the famous composer) and imagine the views that Tchaikovsky would have had of the island of San Giorgio di Maggiore. He didn't necessarily stay in this room, but as just about every room at the Palace shares that view, we can be fairly confident that this was the scene that daily inspired him.

COMMEMORATING FAMOUS GUESTS

Today Tchaikovsky's sojourn at the Beau Rivage is commemorated by a large screen of frosted glass etched with his handwriting inside the lobby of Hotel Londra Palace. The two lions now sit here side by side, rather as if they are waiting for the return of their Russian friend. The hotel has named its restaurant Do Leoni, partly in Tchaikovsky's honour, and also created a bedroom – No. 106 – that bears his name. It's richly decorated in red and gold and features a photo of the composer and various bits of copied memorabilia. No one actually knows where Tchaikovsky stayed in 1877 so Room 106 is more of an homage.

No one knows exactly where the poet Gabriele D'Annunzio stayed in 1887 either, when he attended the unveiling of the monument to King Vittorio Emanuele II that had been built in front of the hotel. Nor indeed the novelist Jorge Luis Borges, who stayed here several times in the 1960s and 70s. They all have rooms named after them but we will never know if these were actually *their* rooms.

One curious footnote for anyone researching the history of the Hôtel d'Angleterre/Beau Rivage/Londra Palace is that it had a fourth name during the Fascist period. Because the authorities felt that 'Londres' and 'Beau Rivage' combined elements of two enemy cultures, the hotel was renamed Bella Riva. Fortunately, since 1973 when the Hotel Londra Palace came into being there have been no further name changes, making the job of the hotel historian so much easier!

GRAND HÔTEL ET DE MILAN, MILAN (1863)

In May 1863 a new hotel named L'Albergo di Milano opened in Milan. The architect was the great Andrea Pazzala (1798–1862) who had died the previous year. Pazzala had designed many important structures in Lombardy including Milan's Galleria de Cristoferis (1831) which was the first commercial *galleria* in Italy, predating the world-famous Galleria Vittorio Emanuele II by 46 years. Sadly almost all of Pazzala's buildings in Milan, even his luxury swimming pool, the Baths of Diana, have since been demolished. Of his Albergo not much remains either. The original inn stood on Corsa del Giardano (now Via Manzoni) but it developed in stages, folding round the corner into Via Croce Rossa and folding again into Via Monte di Pietá. This expansion was slow, held up for some time by the owner of Via Croce Rossa 3, the missing part in the jigsaw, who was running a brothel on the site and had no wish to cease trading.

Eventually all the elements in the hotel were joined up and given a harmonious Neo-Renaissance façade – and a new name. Henceforth the Albergo was to be the Grand

Photo: Geobia

Hôtel et de Milan. This unusual confection of words made sense in Italy where it was possible for an albergo to become a grand hotel of the world and yet still be 'of Milan' in the eyes of locals.

Milan's grandest hotel was managed by a man whose aspirations were as grand as his property. Commendatore Giuseppe Spatz was a highly respected figure in Milan and prominent in moderate politics. During his time he oversaw the installation of the Stigler hydraulic lift system, the creation of a glass-roofed winter garden behind reception, and the establishment of a telegraph and postal office so that important guests need never feel out of contact.

Spatz also courted illustrious guests, a policy that paid off when in April 1888 Dom Pedro II, Emperor of Brazil and his entourage stayed at the hotel on their way south from Venice. In their honour Spatz not only redecorated the royal apartments but transformed the lobby and staircase of the hotel into a tropical garden to make the ailing emperor feel at home. Aged 57, Dom Pedro was in Europe to recover his health. He was feted wherever he went by intellectuals like Darwin, Hugo, Nietzsche and Wagner, all of whom saw him as a civilising force in barbaric South America. While at the hotel Dom Pedro's health deteriorated further and he spent two weeks hovering between life and death. On 22 May, however, the Emperor received news that slavery had finally been abolished in Brazil, something that he had worked decades to achieve. With a weak voice and tears in his eyes, he is said to have declared, 'A great people! A great people!' and that evening he recovered sufficiently to play Chinese Shadows in the hotel ballroom with his wife and courtiers.

In recognition of this momentous news reaching Dom Pedro while he was staying at the Grand Hôtel, Spatz arranged for a statue to be placed in the lobby which showed a half-naked 'Indian' maiden spearing the snakes of slavery writhing round her feet. It can still be seen there today.

In the twentieth century the Grand provided beds for many prestigious visitors to Milan, including – at different times – the sculptor Giorgio de Chirico, film directors Vittorio de Sica and Luchino Visconti, the painter Tamara de Lempicka, the singers Enrico Caruso and Maria Callas, the dancer Rudolf Nureyev and the poet, politician and all-round lover of women and great hotels Gabriele d'Annunzio. Today there are suites named after each.

Yet the guest with which the hotel is most closely associated was a local composer who first stayed here in 1872 while it was still L'Albergo di Milano. Giuseppe Verdi, the most critically and financially successful Italian composer of his generation, had an estate 100 kilometres south of Milan but was often in the city for performances of his work and to visit his publishers who had offices next to La Scala. Verdi used to refer to Suite 105 at the Grand as his 'office', and the hotel displays a handwritten telegram that he handed in to their office to be sent to his adopted daughter Maria Carrara Verdi.

A good relationship developed between Spatz and Verdi, so much so that when Spatz's daughter Olga wanted to marry the young composer Umberto Giordano, the manager appropriated some pages of the opera Giordano was working on for Verdi's opinion. The opera was *Andrea Chénier*. Verdi – wisely – saw great merit in it and so the wedding went ahead. In Verdi's old age he and Giordano often lunched together at the Grand Hôtel.

In 1901 when Verdi lay dying in Suite 105 (now Room 106) such was the clamour for news among his devoted Milanese audience that Spatz posted daily – even hourly – reports of the maestro's health outside the hotel. In response the people are said to have laid straw the length of Via Manzoni to muffle the horses' hooves for their hero.

YET ANOTHER HEMINGWAY STORY

According to hotel legend, Ernest Hemingway taught the bar staff how to mix a martini when he returned to Milan with his first wife, Hadley, in 1922. The legend is obviously just that, as in 1922 Hemingway would have gone unnoticed by the hotel like any other non-celebrity guest.

Hemingway definitely showed Hadley Via Manzoni 10 (now the Galleria d'Italia) where he had fallen in love with his American nurse Agnes von Kurowsky. At the age of eighteen Hem had volunteered as an ambulance driver in the First World War and was sent to the Italian front at Fossalta di Piave in the closing months of the war. Almost as soon as he arrived, he was hit by shrapnel after delivering chocolate to Italian troops, but he managed to rescue one wounded comrade before falling unconscious. Hemingway received a medal for his bravery and spent six months in Milan recovering. During this time he persuaded the 26-year-old Agnes to marry him, but when Hemingway returned to America in 1919 she broke off the engagement, leaving him devastated.

Fortunately Hemingway was always very good at drowning his sorrows.

There is nothing in Hemingway's letters to suggest he drank at the Grand Hôtel et de Milan in 1919, but given its proximity to Via Manzoni 10 it is more than likely. The martini story does not stand up, however.

After Verdi's death, Spatz donated the small red bed in which Verdi died to the composer's country estate in Sant'Agata where it is still on display today. The rest of the room, the nineteenth-century sofas, the deep red drapes, the gilt mirrors and chandeliers, remain as they were in Verdi's time (albeit in a refurbished form).

In the 1930s the Grand Hôtel et de Milan was eclipsed by the new and much larger Hotel Principe di Savoia which opened north of the old city walls. The Principe attracted stellar guests like Edward, Prince of Wales, Henry Ford and the ubiquitous Josephine Baker. Moreover the lofty Principe survived the Second World War intact while in August 1943 the Grand Hôtel was one of many historic buildings in the centre of Milan damaged in RAF raids. By the end of the war it was uninhabitable.

In the 1950s the Grand was reconstructed internally (and inappropriately) to plans by the modernist Milanese architect, Giovanni Muzio, best known for his 1920s Ca' Brutta ('The Ugly House') on Via Moscova. In 1991 Muzio's low ceilings and other anachronistic innovations were removed when the Grand Hôtel et de Milan was restored to its nineteenth-century appearance. Even the old hydraulic lift was brought back into service.

HOTEL EDEN, ROME (1889)

In 1855 when Cavalier Ruffini took his census of Roman hotels for Pope Pius IX, the city was found to possess many small hotels and inns, some dating back to medieval times. There were also several larger hotels, including the imposing Hôtel de la Minerve by the church of Santa Maria Sopra Minerva, converted from a palazzo by a French hotelier, Joseph Sauve, in 1810. It is still there today, albeit with an extra floor or two up top. Two other converted palazzos stood at the base of the Pincian Hill: Hôtel de Russie and Albergo d'Inghilterra (now Hotel d'Inghilterra).

In the 1880s both hotels were managed by Francesco Nistelweck, a Munich-born hotelier. (In Rome Nistelweck was believed to be Swiss because at the time it was assumed that all great hoteliers were Swiss.)

By October 1889 Nistelweck, with the help of Albert Hassler, his future father-in-law, had achieved his dream of striking out on his own, converting a three-storey palazzo on the top of the Pincian Hill into a new 63-bedroom hotel. The palazzo belonged to the Prince of Piombino Boncompagni Ludovisi who also owned Villa Ludovisi nearby, but Nistelweck called it 'my Eden'.

Herr Nistelweck's future wife, Berta Hassler, was responsible for the furnishings. Berta was a daughter of the Swiss family who ran Hotel Hassler in Rome and whose brother-in-law Heinrich Wirth was manager of the Hôtel de la Minerve at the bottom of the Spanish Steps. Despite the size of Europe its hoteliers have always lived in a very small world.

The proximity of the Pincian Hill to Porta del Popolo, the main entrance to the city for carriages arriving from the affluent north, made the location of the Eden attractive to tourists. Being near the recently completed main railway station, Roma Termini (1874) meant that the new hotel was ideally placed between both entrances to the city.

Like other ambitious hotel entrepreneurs of his time, Francesco Nistelweck installed all the new innovations that were proving so popular in hotels across New York, London and Paris: a lift, electric lighting, central heating, and hot and cold running water in all bedroom wash basins.

By 1902 the Eden was making enough money to add a fifth floor to the building. On top of it was a broad terrace overlooking the entire city. At this time the hotel used it to dry the linen sheets and embroidered tablecloths, but when rooftop dining came to Rome in the 1960s it would transform into the much-sought-after Terrazza Restaurant.

Up until 1939 Hotel Eden received its share of the minor rich and the titled who seemed to be forever transiting between Europe's grand hotels. The *Livre d'Or* records names like Princess Teresa of Bavaria, King Alfonso XIII of Spain, Prince Paolo of Serbia, Queen Amelia of Portugal, and Grand Duchess Olga of Russia (proving that not all Russian aristocrats made their home at Hôtel de Russie). One page has the signatures of several members of the prestigious Galitzin family from Russia alongside the actress Eleonora Duse and her sometime lover, the poet, pilot, politician and aficionado of hotel lobbies worldwide, Gabriele D'Annunzio. Between 1919 and 1923 Sigmund Freud paid a number of visits to Rome and stayed at the Eden. His signature, *Prof. S. Freud*, can still be found in the visitors' book.

During the Second World War the signature of Franz von Papen, vice chancellor of the Third Reich and Hitler's ambassador to Turkey was added, as was that of Dino Grandi, Mussolini's foreign minister. Then in 1941 Field Marshal Erwin Rommel appended his name. (In 1945 it was a source of great satisfaction to Rommel's North African rival, Field Marshal Bernard Montgomery, to sign the book on the same page as the Desert Fox when he visited Hotel Eden.) The Eden ended the Second World War as the headquarters of the British military command occupying Rome. Eventually it was passed back to Gianfrancesco Ciaceri, grandson of Francesco Nistelweck, to run.

FEDERICO FELLINI

In the 1960s after the roof of the building was no longer used for drying sheets but had become the celebrated Terrazza Restaurant, the Italian film director Federico Fellini always insisted on conducting interviews at La Terrazza. Fellini, who lived at the bottom of the Spanish Steps in Via Margutta, treated the hotel as if it were an annex of his own home. The concierge knew that if the maestro left his hat, coat and red scarf in the cloakroom that meant that he was expecting guests and his favourite table – with the best view of Villa Borghese and St Peter's – had better be free. Fellini made Rome seem exciting in his eccentric film *La Dolce Vita* (1960) although that movie featured the more brassy Excelsior Hotel on Via Vittorio Veneto. Maybe Fellini didn't want to spoil the Eden by making it too fashionable.

In 1954 the handsome diplomat Prince Raimondo Lanza di Trabia committed suicide by jumping from a second-floor window of the Eden. His death inspired the singer Domenico Modugno to write and record his song 'Vecchio frac' ('The old tailcoat'). Remote on its affluent hilltop, the Eden is the kind of place that songs get written about, even sad ones.

For a while the hotel was part of the Exclusive Hotels by Forte group but then in 2013 Hotel Eden became part of the Dorchester Collection owned by the Sultan of Brunei. In 2015 it was closed for extensive renovations. It reopened in April 2017 decorated with an extraordinary amount of Indian marble worked by Italian craftsmen.

It is hotel policy not to reveal how much the refurbishment cost, but it's infinitely beyond anything Cavalier Ruffini could have imagined.

GRAND HOTEL TREMEZZO, LAKE COMO (1910)

At the end of the 1932 film *Grand Hotel*, Greta Garbo expresses her wish to leave Berlin's Grand Hotel and go to 'Tremezzo, that happy, sunny place'. A hotel by that name sits on the western shore of Lake Como. It is certainly sunny and it is rumoured to have been a favourite of Garbo's. By all accounts it was a happy place too, thanks to the care poured into it by the husband and wife team of Enea Gandola and Maria Orsolini Bolla.

Enea Gandola came from Bellagio where his family had inherited a hotel, the Genazzini (now the Hotel Genazzini Metropole) which he ran for a few years with his brother. In 1900 Enea moved with his wife and children across the lake from Bellagio to Tremezzo to manage Hotel Bazzoni (damaged in the Second World War and subsequently badly rebuilt). Bazzoni was one of a number of small hotels grouped together around Villa Carlotta, the summer home of George, Grand Duke of Saxony.

According to family legend, it was probably Maria who urged the idea of building a hotel of their own on the lake – and not just a hotel, but a grand hotel. The role of women in Europe's grand hotels has tended to be overlooked, but often they were the driving force behind what seemed to be their husband's or father's initiative. Maria came from an artistic family and was clearly drawn to innovation. After

Photo: © Kate Tadman-Mourby

the couple visited the Exposition Universelle in Paris, Enea agreed that their new hotel would have its façade illuminated by hundreds of Edison lightbulbs of the kind they had just seen demonstrated.

Finally in 1907 Enea and Maria bought 80,000 lire-worth of land on the western edge of Villa Carlotta's gardens from the Grand Duke. Construction began on an Art Nouveau hotel designed by architect Constantino Ferrario. Old photographs of work in progress show Maria in her long black dress on-site with her husband and Ferrario.

The hotel opened with a grand reception on 10 July 1910. The building was an imaginative and unusual structure rising up steeply, via two grand metal staircases, from the lake. Inside, everything was white, with wicker furniture on the terraces, while upstairs white monogrammed bed linen was changed twice a day in the en suite bedrooms. The presidential suite was on the first floor, Room 113. The hotel believes that if Garbo did come to stay, this would have been her room and they've renamed it accordingly.

On the *bel étage* there was a ballroom (now Sala Regina) and a reading room (now the business centre) which received the major foreign newspapers daily and had shelves stacked with classics in Italian, French, English, German, Spanish, Russian, and Latin.

Furnishings were by Vittorio Ducrot, one of the most important Art Nouveau designers in Palermo and a famous cabinet-maker. Unusually for its time, the hotel stayed open all year round. It had a staff of 100, including boatmen for sailboats and for motorboats. A small orchestra played daily from 11.00am till midday, from 2.00–3.00pm, from 4.00–6.00pm and then from 8.00pm until midnight. Bills and menus were made out in French, as was then the fashion.

The female staff answered to Maria Orsolini Bolla herself,

including the temperamental Madame Carlotta, the head of wardrobe who took frequent offence at the rest of the staff. It was Maria's job to calm her down and prevent her from following through on her threats to resign. When she discovered that Madame Carlotta was tormented by thoughts of what her husband was up to in Milan while she was working at the hotel, Maria arranged for him to visit for fifteen days every three months, and the situation stabilised.

PAUL VON HINDENBURG

The hotel also hosted General Paul von Hindenburg who was to lead the Kaiser's army in the First World War and eventually become President of Weimar Germany in his last years. It was a rare feat to lure the famously insular Hindenburg to Italy. He spent almost his entire life within Germany as he had no interest in the world beyond, claiming that *Ausland* ('abroad') was of no interest to him. It is not known why he ventured as far as Tremezzo.

There was a dramatic irony in Hindenburg doing the hotel such an honour. The Gandolas, like most of Europe, had no idea what a huge upheaval was about to engulf their world – and their clientele. As one Romanoff prince said to Enea in 1914, 'Monsieur Gandola, we're dancing on a volcano'.

Lake Como had long been fashionable among those who could afford a villa or pension but Hôtel Tremezzo, as it was originally named, offered purpose-built luxury that was secluded, friendly and intimate. Like so many hoteliers of their time, Maria and Enea targeted aristocrats like the Orsini family who had created three popes (Celestine III, Nicholas III, and Benedict XIII) as well as industrialists like the Pirelli family of Milan, and artists like Filippo Tommaso Marinetti, the father of Futurism. They always found room for many minor Romanoffs flitting across western Europe, and for the famously 'sapphic' Baroness Mimi Franchetti Rothschild, who gave 'extremely private parties' on the lake.

On 28 July 1914, following the assassination of Archduke Ferdinand, Germany declared war on Serbia and on 30 July Russia, Serbia's ally, ordered a general mobilisation. Overnight the hotel's Russian and German guests melted away and several British guests found themselves marooned in Europe without access to funds. When Italy entered the war on 24 May 1915, the empty suites were taken over by Milanese nobility who had closed their palaces in the city in expectation of an artillery onslaught.

During the First World War the Gandola family, who had hitherto lived in a private wing of the hotel, moved out when Hôtel Tremezzo was requisitioned as a hospital for 500 wounded Italian soldiers. Fortunately they were on good terms with the Grand Duke of Saxony's superintendent at Villa Carlotta next door. He allowed them to live in Villa Emilia – the library of Villa Carlotta – for the rest of the war.

After the war the hotel was restored to the Gandola family and its wealthy guests returned quickly to a landscape that had been untouched by conflict. In the 1920s Lake Como became a resort for health and sport. A swimming pool was constructed at the front of the hotel and a tennis court behind. Sadly on 2 June 1922 Maria Orsolini Bolla, who had been the motivating force behind the hotel, died at the relatively young age of 54. Enea could not bear to run Tremezzo on his own and he sold it to a consortium of three

Italian businessmen, all of whom had been guests in the years before the First World War.

In the 1930s ownership passed to the Sampietro family, who managed to keep Hôtel Tremezzo open during the Second World War, and extended its appeal into the American market. It was then bought by the De Santis family and in 2014 their granddaughter, Valentina De Santis, was appointed CEO. Valentina has redecorated the hotel in a daringly bright array of colours. By all accounts it seems her devotion to this much-loved hotel is just as strong as that of Maria Orsolini Bolla.

HOTEL CIPRIANI, VENICE (1958)
BELMOND HOTEL CIPRIANI

Very few people can claim to have named a famous hotel, a famous bar, a popular drink, and a meat dish that is now presented all round the world. Such a man – though he was far too modest to own up to it – was Giuseppe Cipriani. Born in Verona but brought up in Germany, Giuseppe trained as a waiter after the First World War. He worked his way up through the Metropole in Brussels and the Excelsior in Palermo until he arrived in 1929 at the Hotel Europa in Venice where, as he himself later put it in his memoirs, he was 'ten feet from a cordage warehouse that would one day become Harry's Bar'.

Giuseppe Cipriani had a wide command of languages: English, French, German and Italian. He also had an original idea: a cocktail bar in Venice that the international set could enter without running the intimidating gauntlet of hotel porters, doormen and concierges. However, he lacked the necessary capital.

Then in 1930, Harry Pickering came into Cipriani's life. Harry was a young American who had been sent to Europe with his aunt to cure his alcoholism. Unfortunately Harry was bored and spent most of his time deteoriating further at the bar of the Europa. When Harry's aunt grew tired of him, she abandoned the young man – and her dog – at the Europa and went off with a gigolo. Cut off from funds, Harry Pickering became even more morose. One day Giuseppe Cipriani, against his own cautious instincts, offered to lend him the princely sum of 10,000 lire. It was out of character for Giuseppe, who had a rule about never lending customers money. In this case, however, it paid dividends. Months later, and after a worrying silence, Harry Pickering came back with 50,000 lire – five times the original sum – gave it to Giuseppe and suggested they open a bar together. 'Let's call it Harry's Bar,' he said.

Giuseppe's wife found the location of this now legendary bar, an old warehouse just fifteen by thirty feet. It overlooked the Grand Canal and was down a dead-end passageway. It was exactly what Giuseppe wanted. He would have no sign. Modest and yet inspired, he wanted people to seek out his bar. The décor was by another regular customer of the Europa, Baron Gianni Rubin de Cervin, who created a bright Art Deco space while Giuseppe himself designed the famous three-legged tables, making them as small as possible so guests did not feel hemmed in.

Opened in 1931, Harry's Bar was a huge success. Writers, aristocrats and movie stars squeezed in through its narrow double doors. Harry Pickering was not involved with the day-to-day running of the bar. As Giuseppe put it, Harry was 'without a doubt his own best customer'. Eventually he sold his share of the bar to Giuseppe, who found he didn't have to raise a huge sum at all once Harry's tab was deducted.

At the end of the Second World War, Giuseppe Cipriani narrowly avoided being shot in German reprisals for a partisan attack on Ca' Giustinian, the Wehrmacht headquarters on the Grand Canal. Giuseppe had not been involved, but all those executed were prominent locals whose deaths might discourage other insurgents. In April 1945, alarming amphibious vehicles brought the first New Zealand troops up the Grand Canal past Harry's Bar. Soon after that, the US commander of Allied forces in Venice summoned Giuseppe. 'Cipriani, you are not a good Italian,' he told him. 'You have not re-opened Harry's Bar.'

In 1936 Giuseppe had bought a *locanda* (farmhouse) on the nearby island of Torcello, which he turned into a guesthouse after the war. Ernest Hemingway became a frequent guest on this tranquil spot. Hemingway discovered Harry's Bar in 1949 and now spent a lot of time at Giuseppe Cipriani's locanda on Torcello as well. 'Hemingway burst into Harry's Bar', Giuseppe's son Arigo recorded. 'He was the only customer to successfully insist that Cipriani drink with him, though on one occasion Giuseppe claimed it took him three days to get over the hangover.' Hemingway liked Harry's Bar so much he put it into his novella *Across the River and into the Trees* (unfortunately not a critical or commercial success). The next book he wrote, however, *The Old Man and the Sea*, won him the Nobel Prize for Literature. Whenever a customer would point out that Hemingway had given the bar good publicity, Arigo Cipriani would retort, 'You've got it the wrong way round. We gave him good publicity. It is no accident he got the Nobel Prize after he wrote about Harry's Bar, not before.'

Photo: Bjørtvedt

QUEEN ELIZABETH II

In 1960 Queen Elizabeth II visited Cipriani's locanda on Torcello in a private capacity with the Duke of Edinburgh, who had been a regular at Harry's during his Royal Navy days. The Queen had wanted to dine with the locals, in the way that her husband had, but Italian security forces insisted the locanda be closed for the day. So Giuseppe hired in trusted friends to pose as ordinary Venetians dining at the hotel.

The years after the war brought great prosperity to Giuseppe Cipriani. Orson Welles was a regular guest (often forgetting to pay his bill; on one occasion he was chased down the platform at Santa Lucia station by Arigo). Truman Capote was another; so were the Aga Khan, Barbara Hutton, Aristotle Onassis, and Maria Callas.

In 1948 Giuseppe had invented a drink that combined his favourite fruit, white peaches, with prosecco. He called it a Bellini because its pink colour reminded him of a saint's robe he had seen in a Bellini painting. In 1950 he invented carpaccio for a favourite customer, Contessa Amalia Nani Mocenigo, who had been told she must not eat cooked meat for several weeks. Giuseppe named it after the artist Vittore Carpaccio whose paintings often contrasted whites and vivid reds.

After three world-famous ventures that bore other people's names – Harry's Bar, the Bellini, and carpaccio – Giuseppe Cipriani finally created an enterprise that would bear his own name. In 1953 he bought a piece of land across the Giudecca Canal that had once been a shipyard but was now used for fattening pigs. With its views across the lagoon and to Palladio's church of San Giorgio di Maggiore, the site had great potential, but Giuseppe did not have the capital to transform it until Lord Iveagh, the owner of Guinness, came to dine in November 1956. The two men got talking and the Irishman asked to see the site the next day. Despite the bad weather, Lord Iveagh agreed to fund the project and in April 1958 Hotel Cipriani opened. Three wings were built, variously facing the lagoon, San Giorgio and San Marco – and they were named after their views. The same discreet qualities that made Harry's a success made the Cipriani thrive. In the 1960s guests never signed for drinks or meals. The staff kept a subtle tally, and the kind of guests who stayed at the Cipriani never challenged the bill.

In 1967 when Lord Iveagh died at the age of 93, Giuseppe was unable to buy out the Guinness family so he sold them his shares in the Cipriani. In 1968 the Guinness family sold on the hotel to Sea Containers whose president James Sherwood put it under his Orient Express brand name. With the revived train route from Paris terminating in Venice, the Cipriani soon became the perfectly situated end destination for one of the most glamorous rail journeys in the world.

Today, with its extensive tranquil gardens, the Cipriani is the antithesis of the crowded Harry's Bar but just as much of a Venetian institution.

GREECE

HÔTEL GRANDE BRETAGNE, ATHENS (1873)

The Hôtel Grande Bretagne has seen revolutions and wars, Nazi occupation, the dictatorship of the colonels, the frequent deposition of Greek monarchs, riots during the economic crisis of 2008, and even an act of sabotage that almost killed Winston Churchill on Christmas Day 1944.

It was that all-important matter of location that placed it close to national events. The hotel on La Place du Palais Royal started life as a private mansion opposite the palace of Otto, the first king of the newly independent Greece. The Dimitrou Mansion was constructed in 1842 by a businessman from Trieste. The following year the royal palace was completed. These two buildings formed two sides of what was to become Constitution Square, now Syntagma Square, the focal point of political life in Athens ever since.

Thirty-one years later, in 1873, Mr Stavvas Kentros owned a small Athenian hotel that he had called Grande Bretagne in the hope of attracting British tourists. When he heard that the French Archaeological School was moving out of Dimitrou Mansion, Kentros obtained the lease and converted it rapidly into as imposing a hotel as he could afford.

The new Hôtel Grande Bretagne and the royal palace were the tallest buildings in what was still a very low-rise capital city. In 1879 Kentros took on a partner, an ambitious young man called Efstathios Lampsas who had been a cook in the royal palace. Lampsas, who had studied catering in Paris in the early 1870s, is now looked upon as the father of modern Greek hoteliery. The two men shared a vision. Athens was growing rapidly and urgently needed a respectable – even distinguished – place to stay. By 1885 the partners were able to purchase the Dimitrou Mansion outright. Three years later in 1888, after Stavvas Kentros's death, Lampsas bought out his widow's shares and as sole proprietor made the hotel central to Athenian life.

In 1891 he opened a luxury restaurant (emulating what Ritz was doing at London's Savoy). He also inaugurated dinner dances in Athens and offered his hotel as a headquarters for the committee overseeing the first modern Olympic Games in Athens in 1896. Lampsas continually expanded the footprint of his hotel with the assistance of six of Greece's biggest banks. By the time he died in 1923 and his son-in-law Theodoros Petrakopoulos took over, the Grande Bretagne was beginning to rival the splendour of the neighbouring royal palace.

In 1918 Efstathios Lampsas had employed the Swiss architect Vogt to redesign the exterior of the hotel in a less historic style, in a manner not unlike the current façade but with unusually long ionic columns spanning three of its floors. Unfortunately Greece was entering a turbulent time, with a disastrous war brewing against the remnants of the Ottoman Empire under Kemal Atatürk. The redesign never happened, but the French historian and journalist René Puaux, reporting on the Balkan Wars from Athens, wrote glowingly: 'After the Parthenon, the building in Athens best known to foreigners is the Hôtel Grand Bretagne.'

Between 1924 and 1936 there were eleven military coups and two military dictatorships in Greece. Given its position just next to the royal palace, it isn't surprising that the

Photo: Andrzej Otrębski

Athenian archives are full of photographs of soldiers and field guns outside the hotel.

CHANGING TIMES

Grande Bretagne's records from the 1920s show that the average stay was 20–21 days per visitor and that wars in Europe and the Balkans dramatically changed the profile of the clientele. The hotel had previously been an almost exclusively male environment for business and politics, but in the 1920s families who had lost their homes in the various battles took up residence in the Hôtel Grande Bretagne.

Responding to changing times, Theodoros Petrakopoulos imported an ice-making machine from the US and new Art Deco furniture by Julius and Josef Herrmann of Vienna. The Grande Bretagne was an oasis of calm in troubled times.

In 1940 Greece entered the Second World War when it declared war on Italy. Theodoros Petrakopoulos, now sole owner of the hotel, was one of many democratic Athenians arrested during the state of emergency that followed the outbreak of war. Petrakopoulos was a supporter of the parliamentarian Venizelos rather than pro-royalist dictator Metaxas whose star was in the ascendant during what was known as the National Schism.

Fortunately Petrakopoulos was released when it was realised that the Grande Bretagne was needed to house the general staff of the Greek army. Anticipating a major conflict, the hotel had built extensive underground shelters during the 1930s. These were linked up easily to the royal palace. Below ground, the two buildings essentially merged and became a nerve centre for King George II's government during the war. Meanwhile British RAF liaison officers, redeployed from the Middle East to Greece in anticipation of a German invasion, lived on the hotel's top floors.

Greece fell to the Wehrmacht in 1941. German troops on motorcycles entered Athens on 28 April and immediately informed Herr Schmidt, the hotel's manager, that his building was now German HQ. Two floors were given over to the Italian high command, but the rest was Wehrmacht territory, with the bill to be sent directly to the Municipality of Athens. King George II himself left Athens two days later, and the city endured some very dark days of resistance and reprisal.

Three and a half years later, in October 1944 the Grande Bretagne changed hands again and now became the headquarters of the British army in Greece. Following liberation, rival Greek factions – left- and right-wing – fought through the city and on Christmas Day 1944 the Grande Bretagne was caught up in the action. Disgruntled partisans tunnelled into the hotel's cellars, intending to blow up the British high command. Enough explosives were laid to bring down the hotel, but then Winston Churchill arrived to meet his officers that day and the attack was called off. Although the partisans wanted revenge on the British, they did not want the responsibility of killing Churchill.

In 1957 the Dimitrou Mansion, at the core of the old hotel, was demolished, and the current hotel façade was created pretty much to Vogt's original design from 1918. The building we see today has stood on this commanding spot since 1873, yet it only really reached its current size and shape 84 years later.

Even more remarkable is that the regal lobby we enter nowadays with its marble floors, Corinthian columns and painted ceilings dates from 2003 (finished in time for the 28th Olympiad the following year). The Grande Bretagne is fortunate to have had very few owners and for those owners mostly to have shared the Kentros/Lampsas vision of Athenian grandeur. You'd never guess that up until 2001 there was a very nasty mezzanine floor lowering the lobby ceiling in an attempt at 'modern' ambience.

After an investment of something in excess of 100 million euros, the Grande Bretagne now looks just like the hotel that Stavvas Kentros had in mind back in 1873 – but even better.

POLAND

HOTEL BRISTOL, WARSAW (1901)

By the end of the Second World War the Hotel Bristol was one of the few buildings in the historic centre of Warsaw still standing. Being commandeered as a headquarters for the occupying German forces had conferred some advantages. It was also a recommendation of sorts; the Nazis had a tendency to take over the best hotels.

The hotel was built on the site of the old Tarnowski Palace which the celebrated Polish pianist Ignacy Jan Paderewski had bought as an investment. In 1889 he and his business partner Stanisław Roszkowski thought there was money to be made from a truly up-to-date hotel in a city that was currently third-largest in the Russian Empire.

Paderewski and Roszkowski held a design competition which was won by Stryjeriski and Mączyński who came up with a domed Art Nouveau façade. Deciding he needed something more Neoclassical in keeping with other buildings on Krakowskie Przedmieście, Paderewski brought in a third architect, Władysław Marconi. Marconi's final design incorporated an eye-catching rooftop belvedere to replace the dome. The façade would display an innovative electric-powered clock on its exterior, only the second public clock in Warsaw. The hotel's interior was more radical than its exterior, with many of the public rooms decorated by the great Otto Wagner from Vienna, who created here one of the first wholly Art Nouveau/Jugendstil interiors in a European hotel. Wagner's Sala Kolumnowa dining room and his Bedroom 109 were considered to be some of the finest Jugendstil rooms ever built. The hotel's biggest triumph, however, was a 'crystal lift' made of glass framed in white-painted iron with armchairs for guests to relax in on the way to their rooms.

Practical innovations included a vacuum system housed in the roof that sucked dust from under the hotel carpets and expelled it into the sky. The Bristol also employed one of the first central heating systems in Warsaw. Two eight-seater horse-drawn carriages took guests to and from the railway station, a novel but necessary innovation in a city that had neither taxis nor trams in 1900.

EDVARD GRIEG

Two weeks before the official opening of the hotel it hosted a group of musicians who were attending the opening of the new Philharmonic Hall: German composer Richard Strauss, Italian tenor Enrico Caruso and Hungarian violinist Leopold Auer. The Norwegian Edvard Grieg was also invited and agreed to attend despite his fears over visiting such a backward part of Europe. He cabled Raichman, the director of the Philharmonic Hall: 'Coming. Please find me a room without bed bugs. Grieg.' When he was escorted into the glittering Jugendstil lobby of the Bristol, he turned to director Raichman and said, 'I am sorry, I am very sorry.'

The hotel was given a Catholic blessing on 17 November 1901 and opened two days later. There were 200 bedrooms in a variety of decorative styles, 80 of which were suites but only twenty of which had their own bathrooms.

In 1907 the Bristol held its first New Year's Ball, destined to be a regular event whenever Poland wasn't caught up in other people's wars. In 1913 it hosted Madame Curie, who was delighted and visibly moved to be able to give a lecture for the first time in her life in her native Polish rather than French. The hotel prospered in the years before the First World War and was poised to bring in real profits for Paderewski and Roszkowski when Germany's conflict with Russia spilled over into Poland. Warsaw was occupied from 4 August 1915 until the German surrender in November 1918. The Kaiser's army tried to requisition the entire hotel but settled for a quarter of it, plus the dining room. Inevitably they damaged the place and paid less than the going rate. Occupying armies are rarely the best customers. By 1917, when Germany ceased fighting on its Eastern Front, the Bristol was heavily in debt, looking rather tired and making only a quarter of its turnover at the beginning of the war.

The turbulent years that followed the Russian Revolution of 1917 led to the establishment of an independent Polish Republic with Paderewski – who had ceased performing in order to lobby for a free Poland – as Prime Minister. Unfortunately the Polish–Soviet War (February 1919–March 1921) that stopped the westward spread of Bolshevism at the massive Battle of Warsaw, made the business of running a hotel nearby very difficult. Government wasn't much easier. By the end of 1919 Paderewski had resigned from both and left Poland never to return. The new management set about modernising the Bristol, which meant that over the next three years running water was installed in all bedrooms but much of the Bristol's Jugendstil beauty was destroyed.

By the mid-1930s the hotel was reaping the benefits of surviving the Depression and became a hub of social life in Warsaw. The hugely successful Polish artist Wojciech Kossak rented its top floor as his studio. He recorded that when President Moscicki came to have his portrait painted in 1934 all the bellboys were given new uniforms and lined up for his inspection. Moscicki picked up the smallest, whom he took to be the youngest, and kissed him on both cheeks only to discover that the object of his affection was an adult dwarf.

Dark years followed the German invasion of Poland in 1939, which the western European powers did too little to prevent. On 1 October when German soldiers entered the Hotel Bristol to make it '*nur für Deutsche*' (Germans only), a Polish soldier stood up and shouted 'I will never surrender!' and shot himself. The Warsaw Uprising against the Wehrmacht in 1944 was also insufficiently supported by the western Allies, and effectively sabotaged by the Red Army. Its failure led to Adolf Hitler's order to erase Warsaw from the map. *Verbrennungs und Vernichtungskommando* (Burning and Destruction Detachments) went to great lengths to exact the Führer's revenge when they could have more usefully been employed fighting the Allies. Remarkably, Hotel Bristol survived the city's destruction pretty much intact. But more suffering was to follow as Poland's independence was snuffed out by Stalin.

During their years in the Communist Eastern Bloc (1945–90) the people of Warsaw were allowed to rebuild their city exactly as it had been before the war. The reconstruction was done so well it is sometimes difficult for visitors to believe the Second World War ever happened.

Those post-war years were not the best for the Bristol, however. Like many grand hotels, it survived occupation by the Third Reich only to be eviscerated in the name of 'modernisation' in the 1960s. In 1969 the famous Crystal Lift that had survived two world wars was sold for scrap.

In February 1991, three months after the election of Lech Wałęsa as president – and the formal end of the Communist People's Republic of Poland – the privatised Hotel Bristol was closed for a massive and much-needed renovation. It was reopened in 1993 by British Prime Minister Margaret Thatcher, a telling choice of VIP given her implacable hostility towards Communism. In 2001 Marconi's rooftop belvedere reopened for summer meals and guests could once again enjoy views of a truly beautiful (albeit 85 per cent reconstituted) city.

RUSSIA

GRAND HÔTEL D'EUROPE, ST PETERSBURG (1875)
BELMOND GRAND HOTEL EUROPE

Few hotels have had such a dramatic life as this imposing Nevsky Prospekt palace. Its Neoclassical pink and cream façade works hard to give the impression that this is one long, majestic building. In fact it is a composite of many and the hotel's origins are surprisingly humble.

Back in the 1830s two slightly seedy hotels stood here on the corner with Mikhailovskaya Street. One was called Coulon's and the other Klee's. Neither was well-regarded by travellers, but at that time St Petersburg was still emerging from the swamp upon which Peter the Great had built it in 1703, and all visitors to the capital complained about mosquitoes and bed bugs.

When these two hotels were merged in the 1840s to create Hotel Rossiya, standards began to improve and the hotel's ground floor restaurant became a meeting place for writers and critics in the St Petersburg of Tsar Nicholas I.

In 1858 the French poet and critic Théophile Gautier found the hotel bigger and grander than he had expected: 'Its corridors are longer than many roads,' he recorded. The Russian novelist Turgenev was another enthusiast for 'Hôtel de Russie' as the Rossiya was also known. In 1862 he invited Dostoyevsky to dine with him there. It can't have been an easy meeting, as the two writers feuded endlessly. At this time the Rossiya was more popular as a restaurant than as a hotel. The 1867 the *Handbook for Travellers in Europe and the East* referred to St Petersburg as the 'modern capital of Russia' and declared: 'The principal hotels are De France [now the Rock Star Café] and De Russie.'

In 1872 a consortium was formed to turn the Rossiya into an extensive modern hotel. The new building would occupy the same corner site but would incorporate various houses and shops along Mikhailovskaya Street, thereby encompassing an entire city block. The new building was designed with 260 centrally heated bedrooms, a restaurant and pastry shop as well as modern ice-making facilities. Further innovations included kitchen and laundry rooms on the top floor (to make sure no unpleasant smells rose up to bedrooms); pneumatic 'air bells' in every bedroom (pulled once for hot water and twice for a chambermaid); and refuse chutes that allowed rubbish to be emptied directly from each of the hotel's four floors down to the basement.

St Petersburg's new hotel opened in January 1875 as Grand Hôtel d'Europe but it was also known as Europeskaya Gostinnitsa, the Europeyskaya and Hôtel d'Europe, reflecting its international clientele.

Turgenev, previously a loyal supporter of the old Rossiya, now made a point of always staying at the Grand Hôtel when passing through St Petersburg from visiting his mistress in France. On his last visit in August 1881, people literally queued up to visit the Grand Old Man of Russian letters in his room on the third floor. He died two years later in the western suburbs of Paris at the age of 64.

Like so many great hotels, the Grand benefitted from a visionary general manager. From 1901 to 1917 the Swiss hotelier Joseph Wolflisberg-Giger ran the enterprise, enlarging and establishing Restaurant Europe as one of the

Photo: Florstein

most important eating places in St Petersburg with two *maîtres d'hotels*, one Italian, the other French. He also introduced the innovatory German *Tür ohne Luftzug* – a revolving door – at its main entrance, and a caviar bar, as well as building a fifth storey to the hotel with a rooftop restaurant, the Krysa.

MRS AND MRS TCHAIKOVSKY

The composer Peter Tchaikovsky, who had many of his major works premiered in St Petersburg, stayed at Grand Hôtel d'Europe in 1877 on his disastrous honeymoon. Tchaikovsky had married one of his pupils, Antonina Miliukova, but by the time he arrived at the hotel with the intention of presenting his new wife to his family, he had come to detest her. Marriage to a woman was probably not a good idea for Tchaikovsky. The couple spent only two and a half months together but never divorced, probably because the secretly homosexual Tchaikovsky was keen to avoid attracting any scandal.

In February 1917 the Russian Revolution began in St Petersburg with a series of blank shots being fired over the city from the cruiser *Aurora* which was moored in the Neva River. After Lenin's Bolsheviks came to power that November, the Grand Hôtel d'Europe was nationalised, renamed House of Soviet Clerks and had much of its furniture 'liberated'. Dmitry Ryabushinsky, the helicopter pioneer and founder of the world's first Aerodynamic Institute in Russia, was one of many intellectuals and entrepreneurs arrested in his room at the Grand. In 1919 he fled into exile in France.

With tourists reluctant to visit the newly renamed city of Leningrad, the House of Soviet Clerks became a place where delegates to socialist conferences stayed. It also spent some time as a state orphanage. By the 1920s it had become a hotel again, reverting to its old name, Europeskaya Gostinnitsa. In 1928 the American writer John Dos Passos likened its unprepossessing restaurant to New York's Lower East Side, with 'beer, jingly music, white tablecloths, and shoddy whores.'

In 1933 the Europeskaya was made the first Intourist hotel in Leningrad and renamed the National Hotel. Henceforth it received the city's most prestigious visitors. George Bernard Shaw had already stayed in 1931, hoping to find that socialism was triumphing in the Soviet Union. H.G. Wells also stayed at the Europeskaya in 1934 on a similar 'fact-finding' mission.

The Second World War brought appalling suffering to Leningrad. The city endured a 900-day siege following Adolf Hitler's declaration that he would wipe it off the map. In 1941 the hotel became Hospital No. 991, with over 1,300 patients crammed into its 260 rooms. When this facility relocated in 1942, the hotel's remaining staff tried to maintain the building, which mercifully received only one direct hit from German artillery during the entire siege. Miraculously the Europeskaya did survive the Great Patriotic War (as the Second World War is known in Russia), although the rooftop restaurant was so badly damaged that restoration was out of the question.

In 1962 Igor Stravinsky, who had left Russia at the beginning of the First World War, returned to Leningrad and stayed in a suite on the third floor of the hotel. 'No artist's name has been more abused in the Soviet Union than mine,' the composer declared when at the age of 80 he conducted a Russian orchestra for the first time in his life.

It was a significant visit, prefiguring by nearly 30 years the rapprochement of East and West.

With the fall of Communism, much of the hotel's appropriated furniture and fittings were recovered from nearby buildings and the grander rooms, subdivided by Intourist in the 1930s, were restored as suites. In 1991 as Leningrad became St Petersburg once again, the name Grand Hôtel d'Europe was reapplied to the Europeskaya. Fully restored, it soon became a home-from-home of a new breed of rich and famous celebrities visiting Russia – the likes of Elton John, Paul McCartney, and Luciano Pavarotti – as well as modern royalty from all over the world.

HOTEL ASTORIA, ST PETERSBURG (1912)

In the nineteenth century, close to St Isaac's cathedral in St Petersburg there stood an odd-shaped building that occupied a triangular site carved out by converging roads. From the 1870s it was owned by Prince Alexei Lvov, a remarkable aristocrat who not only organised the United Russian Fire Brigade from these premises but also ran a newspaper here called *Pozharnoe Delo*, literally 'The Fire Business'.

In 1910 the Palace Hotel Company of Great Britain, with a view to the Romanoff tercentenary of 1913, bought the site for redevelopment. Working against the clock, they demolished Lvov's three-storey office building and commissioned the German firm Wais and Freitag to build a hotel to rival the Grand Hôtel d'Europe. The design was by Fyodor Lidval, a famous St Petersburg architect of Swedish descent. His façade was decidedly innovative in such a Neoclassical city, a stripped-back form of Art Nouveau that prefigured Art Deco in its angularity.

Named Astoria (as so many hotels with no connection to the Astor family were), St Petersburg's new venture opened in December 1912 just in time to accommodate international visitors for the Romanoff celebrations. Lidval's exterior proved controversial, but the modern interior with steam-driven central heating, an automated vacuuming system, innovative electric call-buttons for room service, and cork soundproofing quickly won over guests. On the ground floor there was a French restaurant, a glass-ceilinged winter garden and a banqueting hall. The partitions between these three could be removed, creating a function room that would seat up to 1,000 visitors.

Among those who read about Lidval's exciting new hotel with enthusiasm at the time was a 24-year-old would-be artist in Vienna. In 1908 Adolf Hitler had been rejected as an architectural student but he continued a lifelong interest in the subject. After his troops invaded Russia in June 1941, he had invitations printed for a celebratory dinner to be held at the Astoria when the Wehrmacht seized Russia's 'Window on the West'.

Before the Führer made his booking, however, the Astoria had a lot of history to live through. In December 1915 Grigory Rasputin, spiritual confidante of the Romanoff family, dined at the hotel with Princess Stephanie Dolgorukaya, wife of a senior official at the imperial court. Like so many of Rasputin's dinners at the Astoria – and at Grand Hôtel d'Europe – it turned into an all-night affair and the Okhrana (secret police) made a detailed report. Rasputin was subsequently murdered in 1916 by a group of aristocrats anxious about his influence over the Tsar and Tsarina.

In 1917, during the Russian Revolution, actual battles

between the Bolsheviks and supporters of the Tsar were fought within the Astoria itself. In March 1919, Vladimir Lenin, leader of the Bolsheviks and chairman of the Council of People's Commissars in the new Federative Socialist Republic, stayed at the hotel and gave a speech from its first-floor balcony. In the ensuing civil war (ending October 1922) the Astoria was transformed into the Petrograd Military Hospital by the Bolsheviks. Finally, with peace, it became the First House of the Petrograd Soviet, in the newly renamed Leningrad, a hotel for foreign visitors where their rooms could be bugged by the Cheka (which had replaced the Okhrana in 1918).

Notable guests of the inter-war years included John Reed, author of *Ten Days that Shook the World*, and Hewlett Johnson, the 'Red Dean of Canterbury', a Fabian cleric, who, like H.G. Wells and George Bernard Shaw, came to Leningrad to observe the triumph of socialism. In 1932 the Russian writer Mikhail Bulgakov, a dissident who was nevertheless under Josef Stalin's capricious protection, stayed at the hotel on his honeymoon. He also recommenced his masterpiece *The Master and Margarita* in Room 412, immediately above the room from whose balcony Lenin had addressed the proletariat in 1919.

In 1941, following the outbreak of the Second World War, the hotel was once again turned into a hospital during the appalling Siege of Leningrad. Writers, artists and musicians trapped in the city were given priority at this most imposing building. Because of Hitler's wish to celebrate his victory at the Astoria, the hotel was not targeted during the bombing of Leningrad.

For decades after the war the Astoria was run by the state-owned Intourist travel group, during which time it was merged with the Hotel Angleterre next door. Both hotels underwent the usual Soviet neglect, which was fortunate for the Astoria. Not too much was ripped out or smothered under a sea of concrete.

TRUMAN FLIES IN

In December 1955 the entire Afro-American cast of Everyman's Opera's *Porgy and Bess* checked in to the Astoria. They were led by George Gershwin's sister-in-law Leonore, whom Truman Capote – accompanying the group – described as 'dripping in diamonds'. Truman in his subsequent book *The Muses are Heard* described how the Soviet-run hotel assigned rooms according to 'Bolshevic logic' so that proletarian painters and carpenters were given better bedrooms than the soloists – or the tame US journalist.

By this time the restaurant, winter garden and banqueting hall were, in Truman's words, 'cavernous affairs and as cheerful as airplane hangars'. The bedrooms were small and over-furnished with 'a miasma of romantic marble statuary'.

In 1987, towards the end of the Communist era, the two hotels were split back into separate ventures and the Astoria was closed for reconstruction. Ten years later, in 1997, the Astoria was bought by Sir Rocco Forte and $20 million was raised to restore the historic interiors and update the workings of the hotel.

Today a remarkable feature of the Astoria is the brass door plates of distinguished guests that are preserved around the lift doors on the ground floor. As well as the usual array of heads of state, opera singers, chess grandmasters, Rolling Stones, and international movie stars like Jack Nicholson and Marcello Mastroianni, there are the names of Russian writers Maxim Gorky and Mikhail Bulgakov as well as Russian musicians Mstislav Rostropovich and Dmitri Hvorostovsky.

Sadly, one name that is not commemorated is Fyodor Lidval himself. By 1918 Lidval's architectural practice had been ruined by the Russian Revolution and he fled to join his family in Stockholm. Although he designed several buildings there, the most fruitful period of his work was over and he died in obscurity in 1945.

TURKEY

PERA PALACE HOTEL, ISTANBUL (1895)
THE PERA PALACE HOTEL JUMEIRAH

In 1883 the Compagnie Internationale des Wagons-Lits began running its Orient Express trains into Istanbul. At that time the best hotels for foreigners were in Beyoğlu, also known as Pera. Christians, diplomats and traders from all over the Mediterranean congregated on this summit across the Golden Horn. In 1892 Wagons-Lits decided to build its own hotel. The architect, Alexander Vallaury came up with a design that was Parisian on the outside but distinctly Ottoman within.

On the ground floor was a ballroom, a shadowy bar and the Kubbeli Saloon illuminated from above by six green glass domes. Pera Palas Oteli opened with a ball in December 1895 and Wagons-Lits's reputation guaranteed it good business. The First World War cut off the supply of European visitors with the exception of German liaison officers but in November 1918 the Europeans returned, and in force. After Germany surrendered, a combined fleet of British, French, Italian and Greek warships anchored in the Bosphorus, and General George Milne, senior British officer in Istanbul, took up temporary residence in the Pera Palace.

The same day a 37-year-old officer from Salonika also checked in. Mustapha Kemal went on to be much more famous than General Milne as Atatürk (Father of the Turkish

Nation). A successful strategist who had led the defence of Gallipoli in 1915, Atatürk was determined to limit the dismemberment of the Ottoman Empire by the victorious Allies. That he was militarily successful is reflected in the fact that the Pera Palace keeps Room 101 as a museum exhibiting memorabilia of their most famous Turkish guest.

In 1919 Prodromos Bodosakis, a Greek Orthodox businessman, bought the Pera Palace from Wagons-Lits. Bodosakis proved to be a very successful proprietor. He was easygoing in the melee of occupying Brits, disaffected Ottomans, German businessmen whose fortunes were in freefall and spies, all of whom congregated in the Pera's notoriously decadent bar. Mehmed Ziya Gökalp the sociologist, poet and political activist, castigated the hotel, describing 'foreign officers feted by unscrupulous Levantine adventurers and drinking and dancing with fallen Russian princesses or with Greek and Armenian girls whose morals are, to say the least, as light as their flimsy gowns'. Not surprisingly the Pera made a lot of money.

By 18 September 1922 Atatürk had ensured that all the occupying armies were expelled. Ernest Hemingway arrived in Istanbul that month to cover the fighting between Greeks and Turks but checked into the Grand Hôtel de Londres. This meant that he missed the drama witnessed by his friend and rival John Dos Passos who came downstairs one day to find that the envoy from Azerbaijan had been assassinated in the Pera's doorway. Dos Passos recorded that there was 'blood everywhere' as beleaguered waiters implored fleeing guests to settle their bills.

In July 1923 the Treaty of Lausanne recognised the newly formed Republic of Turkey. Over a million Greeks fled Turkey for Greece, including Bodosakis, and his hotel was declared 'property of the state'.

Despite being nationalised, the Pera continued to offer dinner with a string quartet every evening. Istanbul remained a heady place after Atatürk's victory. It was normal for guests at the Pera to go on to the Garden Bar in Petit-Champs Park where highwire artists, drag queens, Cossack dancers, and prostitutes of many nations entertained an international clientele.

In 1928 the Pera Palace was sold to a Turkish Muslim called Misbah Muhayyes. The proximity of Istanbul to Europe and the stability provided by Atatürk's new secular republic brought a lot of travellers and writers to the Pera. Agatha Christie stayed here in 1934 and even wrote some of her novel *Murder on the Orient Express* at the hotel. Ever since, the hotel has maintained 411, Christie's room, as a memorial to the author with its original narrow twin beds and uncomfortable stick-like chairs.

In the 1930s the centre of social life under Atatürk's republic moved north to Taksim Square and the hotel went into a slow decline. Perversely, one development that helped the Palace was a Jewish boycott of all German enterprises in Istanbul. This hit Pera's rival, the Austrian-run Tokatlian Hotel, hard and brought business back to the Palace.

In 1939 Joseph Goebbels, Hitler's minister of propaganda, checked into the Pera, and visited Hagia Sophia before lunching at the Teutonia Club. His visit did not persuade Atatürk's successor, President İnönü, to ally with Adolf Hitler.

Turkey's neutrality didn't protect the Pera Palace, however. In 1941 British diplomats expelled from Bulgaria arrived in Istanbul and – naturally – checked into the Pera. As they did, a bomb that had been planted in a suitcase detonated, injuring many in the hotel reception and killing six. The blast caused the elevator to crash down its shaft and blew open the floor of reception. In the smoke and darkness, people fell into the basement, increasing the number of injuries. The hotel closed for repairs and a furious Misbah Muhayyes cabled Winston Churchill for compensation. When this was not forthcoming he sued George Rendell, British ambassador to Bulgaria, for negligence. Muhayyes won in the Turkish courts, but he was unable to use the judgement to get money from London.

GRAHAM GREENE

In 1932 Heinemann published Graham Greene's *Stamboul Train*. Greene, in his late twenties, was in need of a literary potboiler to boost his income. *Stamboul Train*, a thriller about travellers on the Orient Express, delivered sales and was turned into a mediocre film in 1934. At that time Greene had been no further by train than Germany so he had to make up many of the descriptions. When he got to the obligatory scene at the Pera Palace, his hero announces to the heroine that they are going to have dinner there – and the novel resumes afterwards. Later, as his fortunes improved, Greene did stay at the Pera and featured it at length in his 1969 novel *Travels with my Aunt*, where the hotel is described as having 'the appearance of an eastern pavilion built for a world fair'. After drinking raki in the bar 'which was all fretwork and mirrors', Greene's narrator takes 'dinner by myself in the hotel in a restaurant which reminded me of Santa Sophia'.

While the Palace was being repaired, the collection of spies, black-marketers and journalists who propped up its bar had to find new places to meet. After the Second World War the hotel resumed its relationship with travellers on the Orient Express. When scheduled services ceased, the famous route was taken over in 1982 by the luxury Venice–Simplon Orient Express established by hotelier James Sherwood.

In 2006 the hotel closed for four years of extensive renovation. In 2010 it was reopened by the Turkish Demsa Group who brought in Jumeirah as managers. Refurbishment has allowed light to flood in again and restored the hotel's early Parisian-style glamour, but the bright, shiny interior has lost some of its famous loucheness in the process.

AFRICA

MENA HOUSE, GIZA, EGYPT (1886)

In the 1870s Thomas Cook began sending tourists to Egypt. At that time the only suitable hotels for European travellers were in Cairo itself. Shepheard's Hotel had been offering lodgings for those who wanted to see the pyramids since 1841, but it was an uncomfortable fifteen-kilometre journey out to Giza.

The first European hotel close to the pyramids was opened by a middle-aged English couple called Ethel and Hugh Locke King. In 1885 they purchased the Khedive's old hunting lodge from Frederick and Jessie Head, who had bought it as a private residence while on their honeymoon. The Locke Kings immediately set about creating a modern hotel that would rise on a gentle incline in a series of white residential blocks. There would be an elaborate portico and awnings in *mashrabia* (wooden screen) work. The name Mena House was chosen in honour of King Menes, credited with having united Upper and Lower Egypt (c. 3100 BC).

Completing the hotel took some time. Writing in 1885, Karl Baedeker noted that the Bedouins were artfully hindering its completion, 'fearing that this might bring an end to their exploitation of travellers'.

When it did open in 1886 the Mena House had 80 bedrooms with blue tiles, marble and mosaics in the public areas and carved wooden doors. Its style might be called 'Egyptiana' or Orientalism crossed with Victorian comfort.

In those days the hotel closed during the hot summer months (1 May–1 November) but in the warm winter months a coach and four ran from Thomas Cook's offices in Cairo out to Mena House at 11.30 every morning, returning in the afternoon after tea at the hotel. This allowed for about two hours inspecting the pyramids. The trip was popular and had to be booked in advance.

In 1889, Prince Albert Victor of Wales (the oldest son of Britain's future King Edward VII) gave the hotel a royal endorsement by staying there. The following year the Locke Kings opened Egypt's first swimming bath, an open marble pool. This European innovation was emptied every night, cleaned by hand and then refilled for the following morning. (Labour was cheap in those days.) Business was clearly going well, leading Hugh Locke King to announce that henceforth the hotel would remain open year-round, a significant development given that wealthy Europeans did not vary their rigid dress code even in the heat.

In 1894 an Austrian aristocrat called Baron Ernst Rodakowski bought shares in the hotel and took over running it from the Locke Kings. One of his innovations was a Hungarian band that would play every Wednesday and Sunday in the dining hall during lunch, and every Saturday evening on the terrace for dancing.

In 1896 a hotelier called Emil Weckel arrived as manager. By 1898 the enterprising Weckel had bought out Rodakowski and laid plans for an ambitious eighteen-hole golf course. Opened in 1899, the course required an unprecedented level of irrigation and its eighteenth hole was beneath the Great Pyramid. Other hotel activities included gymkhanas, horse racing and polo played on camelback.

In 1900 a tram line was constructed from Cairo to Giza, making the pyramids – and their famous neighbour –

MENA HOUSE, GIZA, EGYPT

Photo: Gerhard Haubold

223

more accessible. Emil Weckel celebrated the new century by building a grand lift tower that might have passed for a minaret on one side of the hotel. He also installed electric lighting on all four floors.

A WARM PLACE IN WINTER

In 1894 Arthur Conan Doyle arrived at the Mena House Hotel in the hope that the warm winter climate would be good for his ailing, tubercular wife. Agatha Christie's first visit to Egypt was with her ailing mother (who was also in need of a warm, dry climate). The year was 1910 and mother and daughter stayed at the Gezirah Palace Hotel in Cairo. However in the 1930s Christie visited Mena House with her archaeologist husband, subsequently setting a crucial early scene in *Death on the Nile* (1938) at the hotel.

In 1904 Weckel and his shadowy business partner, Herr Schick, sold the Mena House to the George Nungovich Egyptian Hotel Company. Nungovich, who began his career as a porter on Cairo station, ended up owning seven hotels in Egypt.

By now Mena House was the hotel where every dignitary who wanted to see the pyramids stayed. This impressive roster included Empress Eugénie, the widow of Napoleon III, and Prince George (England's future George V) who in 1906 was on his way back from a tour of India.

During the First World War the hotel was requisitioned as a barracks for Australian troops. According to hotel legend they brought with them their mascot – the first kangaroo ever seen in Egypt. The marsupial was admitted to the hotel despite a 'no pets' rule. Winston Churchill, Minister of Munitions, also visited Mena House, the first of a number of trips he was to make, including in peacetime and, later still, during the Second World War. As Churchill famously insisted, his attitude to hotels was simple: he was always easily satisfied with the best. The Australians must have been happy too because they requisitioned the same hotel again during the Second World War.

In 1943 when Churchill and Roosevelt needed to discuss the South-east Asian front with Chiang Kai-shek of Taiwan they met him at the Mena House Hotel with approximately 500 anti-aircraft guns positioned around the grounds, just in case. During the conference Madam Chiang Kai-shek surprised the gentlemen by insisting on sitting in on discussions rather than visiting the pyramids as was proposed. With her fluent English she frequently corrected the interpreters.

During the same conference the *chef de cuisine* fell ill and consulted the eminent physician Dr Zaki Souidan, whose practice had grown up close to the hotel and blossomed thanks to the many wealthy guests. When it came time to settle his bill, the chef allegedly presented the doctor with a large jar of caviar, one of three that had been sent over by General Secretary Josef Stalin for Winston Churchill's personal use. 'I thought two were enough for him,' was the chef's excuse.

In 1946 the exiled King Zog and Queen Geraldine of Albania spent seven months at the Mena House after being invited to live in Egypt by King Farouk. The safe containing their worldly wealth was so big it could only be installed in the couple's bedroom by being hoisted up the outside of the hotel and pulled in through a large window. Zog and his half-American consort lived in Egypt until the overthrow of King Farouk.

Farouk fell in 1953 as Egypt was declared a republic. Soon afterwards Mena House Hotel was nationalised. It failed to thrive during the long years between the Suez Crisis of 1956 and the Six Day War of 1967, both of which made Egypt a less attractive proposition for travellers.

In 1972 the Indian Oberoi chain – with the financial backing of Egypt's President Anwar Sadat – took over the running of the hotel and not only restored it but expanded it with a new garden wing.

In December 1977 the newly sumptuous hotel was the venue for the preliminary Cairo Conference that led to the Camp David Agreement of 1978. Menachem Begin of Israel was housed in Room 908, Anwar Sadat in the suite named after Field Marshal Bernard Montgomery, and President Jimmy Carter in the Churchill Suite.

Mena House was back, centre stage in world affairs again.

REID'S NEW HOTEL, FUNCHAL, MADEIRA (1891)
BELMOND REID'S PALACE

When a fourteen-year-old Scots cabin boy called William Reid first stepped ashore on the island of Madeira, he had £5 in savings, a not inconsiderable sum in 1836. After making a fortune in Madeira's flourishing trade in fortified wine, young Mr Reid was ready to invest in property. He could see that north Europeans might want to over-winter on such a warm island. So he bought and converted farms to let to sun-seekers, then he acquired small hotels. Finally in the 1880s the white-bearded Mr Reid realised his dream of building a palatial hotel that would bear his name.

Finding a rocky site west of Funchal, Reid brought in tons of rich soil to create the lush sub-tropical gardens that he envisaged for his Atlantic paradise. The chosen architect was George Somers Clarke, whose reputation had already been established by Shepheard's Hotel in Cairo. Clarke worked with J.T. Micklethwaite whose expertise was in the English Gothic Revival. Construction work began in 1887 but before the exterior was completed in 1888, William Reid had died.

The hotel was opened in November 1891 by his two sons, William and Alfred. At that time, a single room at the hotel cost from £12 for a four-week period and a double room was from £22. A servant's room, with meals, for the same period was £6. Stays tended to be measured in weeks, as it would typically take six days to reach Madeira from England.

At the time the hotel opened, ships arriving at Funchal en route to South Africa or travelling west to the Americas would be met by an armada of small, colourful boats packed with vendors and their wares. Any ship, be it a naval frigate or ocean-going liner, was a big event in the 1890s.

The hotel and its lush gardens created a sensation. By 1894 the Reid's reputation was so impressive that 'Sissi', Empress Elizabeth of Austria and Hungary came to stay. She briefly occupied Villa Vittoria, a house in the grounds, but then moved into the hotel proper. In her honour British naval vessels calling at the island fired a royal salute each morning as the Austrian flag was hoisted.

Captain Scott stayed at Reid's in 1910 en route to the Antarctic, and so did his rival, Roald Amundsen. Another polar explorer, Sir Ernest Shackleton, also stopped off at Reid's when heading south. Indeed, the last known photograph of him was taken on Madeira in October 1921. He died in January 1922, having been taken ill on South Georgia.

Photo: Stefan Bellini

During the First World War the hotel remained shut, as it was difficult and dangerous to attempt the sea-crossing. Although Portugal remained officially neutral, German U-boats did enter Funchal harbour and in 1916 they sank British and French shipping.

The hotel reopened in 1919 with a new manager, Luigi Gandolfo, who had trained at Le Meurice in Paris. He did much to revive its fortunes by extending the Reid's season into the summer. So many British aristocrats took up Gandolfo's boast of 'no rain, no dust' that part of the dining room was nicknamed the House of Lords.

In February 1922, Emperor Charles, heir to Franz Joseph and the deposed ruler of the Austro-Hungarian Empire, was exiled on Madeira with his wife and children. The victorious Allies had sent him to live on this pleasant rock in the Atlantic so he could not spearhead a monarchist movement at home. Initially Charles and Empress Zita lived at Villa Vittoria like his great aunt, but they could not afford Reid's prices long-term so moved to Quinta do Monte, a villa loaned to them by a local banker. Unfortunately it was very damp and in April 1922 Charles died of pneumonia.

In 1924 George Bernard Shaw arrived in Funchal on the liner *Edinburgh Castle*. The self-publicising playwright was 68 years old and intended to spend the next six months working and sunbathing and – so he later claimed – mastering the tango. Shaw later described the hotel's resident dancing instructor Max Rinder as 'the only man who ever taught me anything'.

In 1925, difficulties with their new banking enterprise forced the Reid brothers to sell their hotel. It became the property of an English company called Reid's Palace Hotel (Madeira) Ltd.

In 1937 the Blandy family (partners in what was to become the famous Madeira Wine Company) acquired control of the hotel and made the first substantial changes since it was built nearly half a century earlier. They invested £35,000, adding new wings and two heated sea-water pools.

In 1949 a flying boat service between Southampton in England and Funchal was introduced to speed up the journey time. Eventually an airport opened on the neighbouring island of Porto Santo – although visitors still faced an uncomfortable journey in flat-bottomed boats between the two.

WINSTON'S BOTTLES

Winston Churchill, MP for Woodford in Essex and an inveterate stayer in luxury hotels during his years out of office, arrived at Reid's in January 1950 despite dreadful weather.

While staying at Reid's Churchill painted in the fishing village of Câmara de Lobos, using a Rolls-Royce loaned to him by the Leacock family, partners in the Madeira Wine Company. He also worked on his fourth volume of war memoirs, *The Hinge of Fate*, and suffered a minor stroke. On a visit to Blandy's in Avenida Arriaga (historic home of the wine company), Churchill was pleased to be presented with cases of madeira. The company still have his appreciative letter of thanks on display. They also have his subsequent letters when the long-promised bottles failed to materialise in England, each more testy than the last.

Churchill, his wife and family occupied rooms near the hotel's entrance hall. In his honour these were subsequently renamed the Churchill Suite and have since become one of the hotel's two presidential suites.

In 1955 the hotel was used as a base by John Huston while shooting the Madeiran sequences of his film of *Moby-Dick*, which starred Gregory Peck and provided Orson Welles with a fire-and-brimstone cameo as a New England preacher. Parts of the film were shot at the seafront in Caniçal, thirty kilometres to the east, a traditional community where whaling was still carried out in open-top ships.

That same year Prince Alexander, cousin of the last King of Yugoslavia, stayed at Reid's, as did the deposed Cuban dictator General Fulgencio Batista in 1959 after his defeat by Fidel Castro. In 1965 another former head of state, ex-King Umberto II of Italy, stayed intermittently at the hotel while living in Cascais near Lisbon. Umberto died in 1983 and was the last in a line of dispossessed rulers who were drawn to this rock in the Atlantic, with its warm sunshine, tropical gardens and Mr Reid's remarkable palace.

HÔTEL DE LA MAMOUNIA TRANSATLANTIQUE ET CFM, MARRAKECH, MOROCCO (1925)
LA MAMOUNIA

Not many people who visit La Mamounia today realise how much it owed its existence to the railways. It certainly does not look like your average railway hotel.

Under the French protectorate Morocco's railways began connecting its cities in 1908. They were scheduled to reach Marrakech in the 1920s at the end of a 948-kilometre route that ran from Oujda and Fes down to Casablanca and then Marrakech. As Marrakech was to be the southern terminus, the Office Nationale des Chemins de Fer (ONCF) commissioned a hotel for tourists. The name given to it was Hôtel de la Mamounia Transatlantique et CFM (Chemins de Fer du Maroc).

The name Mamounia came from the site that was chosen within Marrakech's twelfth-century city walls. Here on the northern perimeter stood an *artsat* (garden) that had been given to Prince Al Mamoun of Morocco by his father, Sultan Sidi Mohammed ben Abdallah, in the eighteenth century. King Mohammed was a good, stable ruler, and incidentally the first head of state to recognise the United States of America in 1777. As each of his sons was married off, Sultan Mohammed presented him with an artsat. When Mamoun moved to Fes, however, to become Khalifa, he leased out his gardens commercially.

When ONCF looked at the property 140 years later they found some buildings there, including a nineteenth-century pavilion which was demolished in 1922 to create the hotel. But there was a smaller eighteenth-century pavilion that dated from Prince Mamoun's time. This was retained and after many incarnations is now the hotel's ice cream café.

A number of designs were commissioned from Albert Laprade (1921) and Robert Lièvre (1922) but these were rejected in 1923 in favour of Prost and Marchisio, who also designed Compagnie Algérienne de Credit in Casablanca and Hotel des Îles in Essaouira. Their design ran to 50 rooms on three floors.

In 1925 the hotel opened, with a central block and single wing named 'La Koutoubia'. Inside, Prost and Marchisio provided guests with a mix of the exotic and streamlined modernist design. The French painter Jacques Majorelle, who had moved to Marrakech in 1919 for health reasons, decorated one of the salons. Majorelle later created the Majorelle Gardens in Marrakech, using an intense shade of

Photo: martinvarsavsky

cobalt blue with which he painted the garden's buildings. It is now named after him: *Bleu Majorelle*.

Gradually La Mamounia grew to 100 rooms on three floors under a Moorish-tiled roof. It was filled with wide corridors, fountains, balconies, intricate wooden screens and traditional Moroccan tiling alongside Art Deco furniture from the Vienna School. The main corridor was a series of spacious drawing rooms supported by 25 columns of rectangular Carrara marble. The design of La Mamounia forged a style followed by Moroccan luxury hotels and *riad* conversions for decades.

Many of the early visitors were French, as until 1956 Morocco remained a French protectorate (a colony with a certain level of sovereignty). By 1929 Maurice Chevalier, Edith Piaf and the insatiable Josephine Baker had stayed.

MOROCCO AND MARLENE

In 1930 the recently concluded Rhif War between Moroccan Berbers and the French provided a background for the film *Morocco*, directed in Hollywood by Josef von Sternberg. His protégée Marlene Dietrich starred as the nightclub singer who memorably follows Gary Cooper and his legion barefoot into the desert in the closing scenes.

Although set in Mogador (Essaouira) and entirely filmed in California, it's a popular myth that much of the film was shot in Marrakech and that Marlene Dietrich stayed at La Mamounia while filming. Even though she didn't, it's most likely she visited eventually. Dietrich had a homing instinct for luxury hotels.

In 1935 Winston Churchill visited Marrakech for the first time during his 'wilderness' years out of politics when he was, among other things, a jobbing journalist. After travelling down from Tangier he stayed at La Mamounia and wrote in the *Daily Mail* that he was captivated by Marrakech: 'Here in these spacious palm groves rising from the desert the traveller can be sure of perennial sunshine, of every comfort and diversion, and can contemplate with ceaseless satisfaction the stately and snow-clad panorama of the Atlas Mountains. The sun is brilliant and warm but not scorching; the air crisp, bracing but without being chilly; the days bright, the nights cool and fresh.'

Churchill returned to Marrakech with Franklin Roosevelt during the Second World War after the Casablanca Conference of 1943. On this occasion they stayed privately at Villa Taylor, owned by a Republican couple who were not best pleased to learn that a Democrat president had been their house guest. It was on this occasion that Churchill told Roosevelt that Marrakech (not La Mamounia, as is sometimes claimed) was 'one of the most beautiful places in the world'.

In retirement Churchill returned on a number of occasions to paint in the gardens of La Mamounia. During one of its many refurbishments the hotel bar was posthumously renamed in his honour.

After the Second World War, American and European tourism to Morocco increased, partly encouraged by a number of films that glamorised Marrakech. In 1953 Eric von Stroheim played a villain in *Alarm in Morocco* and is believed to have stayed in La Mamounia while filming. The following year Yves Allégret directed *Oasis* with Michèle Morgan, also set in Morocco, with cast and crew most definitely staying at La Mamounia.

In 1956 Alfred Hitchcock began principal photography of *The Man Who Knew Too Much* with James Stewart on location in Marrakech. During filming Hitchcock and his stars stayed at La Mamounia and filmed its exterior. The production then moved on to London, and finally to Hollywood where Mamounia interiors were created on a sound stage. (This explains why *every* bedroom window seems to have a view of the Ktoubia mosque.)

Although today La Mamounia is on the international celebrity circuit – Sarah Jessica Parker stayed in one of its villas while filming the lamentable *Sex and the City II* (2010) – it has a long and continuing history of attracting the chic and serious from France, including writers and artists like Colette, Maurice Ravel, Georges Duhamel, Paul Valéry, Marguerite Duras, Pierre Balmain, and Yves St Laurent. Ravel is said to have played the hotel piano, and it's claimed that when General de Gaulle came to stay, a specially long bed had to be made to accommodate him (this is probably true, as several hotels make the same claim). What is certainly true is that after visiting La Mamounia and Marrakech, Yves Saint-Laurent and Pierre Bergé bought the Majorelle Gardens in 1980. Saint-Laurent's ashes were scattered there after his death in 2008.

Over the years the hotel has been expanded frequently, redesigned often and has even gained an extra floor. In 1986 it was extended to 179 rooms, 49 suites and four villas, including a wood-panelled Churchill Suite, which has his hat, walking stick, umbrella, brushes, easel and several sketches on display. The most satisfactory refurbishment so far was by Jacques Garcia in 2009, in which he reduced the number of rooms and managed to perfect the synthesis of Art Deco and Moroccan craftsmanship.

CECIL HOTEL, ALEXANDRIA, EGYPT (1929)
STEIGENBERGER CECIL HOTEL

Wrapped in scandal and intrigue, the Cecil Hotel in Alexandria has enjoyed a relatively short but colourful life. It was built in 1929 for Albert Metzger, a Jewish businessman in Alex. Metzger was from Alsace but took British citizenship in 1914, as this made his life much easier than holding a German passport during the First World War. The hotel is located on a glamorous Belle Époque corner of the Corniche.

The chosen architect was Alessandro Lorizdo, another Jewish Egyptian. Lorizdo designed a number of banks and hotels in Alexandria between the wars, but Metzger's graceful new Regina Palace with its Venetian crenellations and balconies was the architect's greatest triumph. Less than a year after the opening in 1929, Metzger changed the name to Cecil Hotel, constructing a large metal sign to that effect on the roof. Renaming his new venture after the largest commercial hotel in London was a wise move. Although Egypt had gained independence in 1922, there was a strong British presence in the country still, especially in Alex.

Within a few years, the new European hotel in the heart of Alexandria had become famous for parties and assignations. Its clientele were wealthy and cosmopolitan: Italians and French, Greeks and Armenians, Jews, Arabs, and of course the British. Metzger's constant attention to detail turned the Cecil, as it was always known among expats, into one of the most famous meeting places in the Levant. Somerset Maugham visited in December 1929, soon after the opening, on a trip to celebrate the completion of his novel, *Cakes and*

Ale. The hotel has also claimed that Al Capone visited – the gangster certainly did like a good hotel – but that would have to have been very soon after its opening. By 1932 he was back in prison, and when he emerged in the 1940s he was in no fit state – physical or mental – to travel.

Albert Metzger was very proud of his showcase property. Though he went on to own six other hotels in Alexandria, the Cecil was where he lived, in a private apartment on the first floor with his family.

The years up until 1939 were glamorous, and the Second World War brought an additional, if unwanted level of excitement with General Dudley Clarke's A Force based in another first-floor suite. From there they worked on a master plan of deception to convince Rommel's Afrika Korps that the Eighth Army was much bigger than it actually was, particularly so in places where the British really didn't want them attacking. On several occasions it looked as if Alexandria would be overrun by the Afrika Korps, but they were stopped for good at the Battle of El Alamein in 1942.

The British novelist Olivia Manning lived in Alexandria for part of the war and visited the Cecil one unusually quiet night: 'Even the bar, the venue of British naval officers was empty except for three army captains who stood together, constrained and sober.' The emptiness of the bar was such an anomaly that Manning put the event into her Levant Trilogy.

Among those who stayed at the Cecil during these heady times were the familiar figure of Winston Churchill, who liked being near a battlefield and always enjoyed a good hotel, and General Bernard Montgomery. The architect of Rommel's defeat was a committed teetotaller, one of the few healthy drinkers to have crossed the Cecil's inner patio. Ironically, the hotel bar was subsequently named after him.

LAWRENCE DURRELL AND THE CECIL HOTEL

If ever a writer immersed himself in a city and its premier hotel it was the Indian-born English novelist Lawrence Durrell, who served as a press attaché to the British embassy in Alexandria during the Second World War.

Separated from his wife, Durrell became involved with an Alexandrian called Eve Cohen. She became the model for Justine, the heroine of what eventually became Durrell's Alexandria Quartet. Justine meets her lover (repeatedly) at the Cecil. Durrell describes her as 'waiting, gloved hands folded on her handbag, staring out through the windows upon which the sea crawled and sprawled, climbing and subsiding, across the screen of palms in the little municipal square which flapped and creaked like loose sails.'

The lobby mirror in which Justine used to check her reflection disappeared during a post-war remodelling of reception. Durrell married Eve in 1947 and they separated in 1955. In 1957, the first novel in the quartet that celebrated Eve Cohen, *Justine*, was published.

Lawrence Durrell was shortlisted for the Nobel Prize for Literature but the committee noted that his Quartet 'gives a dubious aftertaste ... because of [his] monomaniacal preoccupation with erotic complications'.

After the war the Cecil once again attracted Alexandria's wealthy cosmopolitan elite. However, after a revolution by the Free Officers Movement in July 1952 it was nationalised. In 1956, following the Israeli invasion of Sinai, Albert Metzger

– like many Jewish businessmen in Egypt – was given a week to get out of the country. After his expulsion, Metzger began a new life with his family in Tanzania. In Dar Es-Salaam, he bought the New Africa hotel, which he also lost when that too was nationalised after independence in 1964. He died in 1971 leaving his son (also called Albert) and his daughter-in-law, Patricia, fighting for years to get the Cecil back. When they were finally awarded it in 2007, Patricia Metzger immediately sold it back to the Egyptian government for US$10 million minus money for various improvements that had been made in the interim by the state-owned Egoth hotel chain. As these included the destruction of the inner patio, leaving just a small unatmospheric lobby, it must have been particularly galling to have to pay for that 'improvement'.

Fortunately the double metal-gated lifts had survived and Patricia Metzger – whose engagement party had been held in the hotel in 1955 – was able to find the gold-rimmed hotel guest book that had been hidden by her father-in-law.

Today the Cecil's charm lies in the fact that it never was entirely modernised. It lacks real glamour but the glamour of Alexandria lay in the hedonism of its cosmopolitan elite and they left in 1956.

INDIA

THE TAJ MAHAL PALACE HOTEL, BOMBAY (1903)
THE TAJ MAHAL PALACE HOTEL, MUMBAI

There's a common creation myth about hotels: the owner built it simply to spite a rival. The Waldorf and the Astoria on New York's Park Avenue were supposedly constructed next to each other by feuding cousins, William Waldorf and John Jacob Astor, each keen to build higher than the other. The Majestic in Harrogate was allegedly built by Sir Blundell Maple who, after being overcharged at Queen's Hotel in High Harrogate, vowed he would build his own hotel to put Queen's out of business. The Taj in Mumbai is often said to have been built by Jamsetji Nusserwanji Tata because he had been refused entry to Watson's Esplanade Hotel thanks to a 'whites only' policy.

All these stories – and many more like them – ignore the fact that successful business owners know better than to let personal pique propel them into such a financially risky enterprise as building a hotel.

Besides, by all accounts, J.N. Tata was a far from vengeful person. The Watson's story plays to a postcolonial narrative of the arrogant English outwitted by the plucky native. It's far more likely that Mr Tata was inspired by an editorial in the *Times of India* that insisted that Bombay (as it was then known) at the end of the nineteenth century deserved a hotel worthy of its position as the premier trading port of India.

In 1898 the British authorities were already draining the area around Apollo Bunder, the coastal tip south of the Great Indian Peninsula Railway's Victoria Terminus. Here Mr Tata's Indian Hotel Company (IHC) began digging 40-foot foundations to support a new five-storey hotel that would back on to the shore. The architect was W.A. Chambers who had designed the Esplanade Hotel that Thomas Watson had built in the 1870s. For IHC he came up with a much less European design that fused Mughal minarets and Rajput window masonry with a dome straight out of the Florentine Renaissance. The interior had a lofty cathedral-like quality found in so many Victorian railway hotels of the time, combined with practical lightwells and broad-balconied corridors, but its Indian décor was so lavish it tipped the hotel into exoticism. The builder was Khansaheb Sorabji Ruttonji and it was he who was responsible for constructing the much-lauded 'floating' staircase that rose up through the building with no obvious means of support.

The new Taj Mahal Palace Hotel was designed to give Europeans disembarking in Bombay their first taste of India and to give India's princely class a residence in Bombay where they'd be offered the kind of palatial luxury they enjoyed at home. Before it opened Mr Tata toured Europe and America to bring to Bombay all the latest hotel innovations – electric lights, fans and clocks in bedrooms, four passenger lifts, and an ice plant that provided air conditioning as well as ice for drinks. The hotel also offered a resident doctor, a dispensing chemist shop, English butlers and a Turkish bath.

The Taj opened quietly in December 1903. It charged thirteen rupees per night for a superior room with electric fan and en suite bathroom. Full board was available for a further seven rupees. These were significant amounts at the time.

In May 1904 Jamsetji Nusserwanji Tata died and the

running of Bombay's premier hotel – and the rest of the Tata Group's enterprises – was taken over by his son Dorabji. By October 1904 the Taj's first Maharajah had come to stay. Dorabji was able to report not only that the Maharajah was satisfied with the levels of service, but that he was returning in two months' time with his entire retinue.

In these early days the hotel's main entrance and its two wings faced inland, away from the port across a large apron (where the swimming pool is situated today). Attitudes to stretches of natural water changed in twentieth-century Bombay, just as they did in Venice, where rooms overlooking the Grand Canal were originally cheaper because of the noise and the smell below.

During the First World War there was a plan to requisition the hotel as a hospital. This happened at the nearby Prince of Wales Museum and the Royal Institute of Science, but the Taj Mahal Palace successfully proposed that it could serve the war effort better by providing accommodation for officers on leave in Bombay at reduced rates.

In 1924 the construction of the Gate of India on the harbourside increased the perceived importance of what had been the back of the hotel and the main entrance was moved round. The 1920s and 30s were a good time for the Taj – princes, presidents and prime ministers came to stay, as well as movie stars and literary luminaries like the positively nomadic Somerset Maugham, and Aldous Huxley who took an instant dislike to most of Bombay's architecture. In 1933 Mumbai's first-ever licensed bar for guests and non-guests alike was created at the Taj (today's Harbour Bar).

The hotel remained a family business, with the youngest son of Ratanji Dadabhoy Tata, Sir Dorabji's cousin, actually born at Taj Mahal Palace in 1914. Ratanbai Petit Jinnah, granddaughter of Ratanji Dadabhoy Tata, lived out her last

Photo: Mintu500px

days at the hotel, dying in 1929. She was the estranged wife of Muhammad Ali Jinnah, the future Father of Pakistan.

HUXLEY ARRIVES BY SEA

Aldous Huxley wrote about visiting Bombay in his book *Jesting Pilate: India and Burma* (1948). The author of *Brave New World* did not much like his first impressions of the city and objected to Parsi women on the quayside whom he considered 'all ugly'. However, he did warm to the Taj Hotel:

'Architecturally Bombay is one of the most appalling cities of either hemisphere [but] the gigantic Taj combines the style of the South Kensington Natural History Museum with that of an Indian pavilion at an International Exhibition.'

In 1947 India became independent. In June 1948 when Lord Louis Mountbatten, the first Governor-General of independent India, gave his farewell speech, it was delivered in the Taj ballroom, after which he boarded ship in the harbour and sailed home.

That same year there was another moment of drama when the Maharajah of Kathpurthala died in the Taj. According to the practices attending on an Indian prince, he had to be carried out of the Taj respectfully, which meant sitting upright in a chair.

In 1949 plans to demolish the ageing building and replace it with a modern yacht club and hotel were met by citywide protests and the following year any such destructive ideas were permanently shelved. By the 1960s, however, the Taj was looking very run-down. Its revival began in 1973 with the creation of the Taj Mahal Tower, a freestanding additional wing. The juxtaposition of three very different buildings, the Tower, the Palace and the Gate of India, make for an iconic grouping.

Also in the 1970s the Tata Group created Taj Hotels, Resorts and Palaces that built new hotels and converted palaces into hotels. The Taj on Apollo Bunder was its flagship.

In 2008 the Taj Mahal Palace Hotel was attacked by Lashkar-e-Taiba, a Pakistan-based terrorist organisation. One hundred and sixty-seven people were killed over a three-day battle with the Indian army that destroyed much of the hotel, including its famous roof. The Taj Mahal Tower defiantly reopened within a month and the rest of the hotel successively during 2009 and 2010.

The attack was viewed nationally and internationally as a blow against the prosperity and liberal values of Indian society via one of its most famous hotels. It was also aimed at deterring western tourists – which it failed to do. Today in a corner of the main lobby there is a memorial with 32 candles to honour those who died in the hotel. But the Taj's continuation is a memorial in itself, particularly to the ideals of Jamsetji Nusserwanji Tata who eschewed any ideas of revenge or anger in search of progress and prosperity.

THE IMPERIAL HOTEL, DELHI (1936)

The Imperial Hotel holds an important place in Indian history but the guidebook that states that Nehru, Gandhi, and Jinnah agreed the Partition deal in its bar misrepresents the facts. Nevertheless the myth persists. The idea of the Mahatma and Nehru sitting with their glasses of orange juice

while Jinnah sips his whisky and Lord Mountbatten sketches out the details of independence on the back of an envelope has its humorous side. It was actually in the hotel's ballroom that Partition was discussed and finally agreed in June 1947.

That the Imperial Hotel was chosen for such crucial discussions says a lot about how far the grand hotel in India had risen to a position of respectability – and neutrality – from its origins. The days of John Watson's 'whites only' Esplanade Hotel in Bombay (built in prefabricated sections in England and constructed 1867–69) were long in the past.

The building of this new hotel in Delhi was championed between the World Wars by the formidable Marie Freeman-Thomas, Marchioness of Willingdon and wife of the Viceroy. The Marchioness saw a modern hotel as an important missing element in Edwin Lutyens' great plan for New Delhi. She observed that the British ladies of New Delhi didn't have somewhere suitable to meet socially. A hotel offered the ideal solution. At her urging a location had been reserved for a hotel on Queensway (now known as Janpath), one of the boulevards that connected Connaught Place with Viceroy's House (now Rashtrapati Bhawan).

The architect was Charles G. Blomfield, one of Edwin Lutyens' assistants on the New Delhi project, who also built several houses in what is now known as the 'Lutyens Bungalow District'. The builder was S.B.S. Ranjit Singh whose family still owns and runs the hotel. The Singh family had been involved in constructing some major projects during British rule. In fact R.B.S. Narain Singh, father of the hotel builder, had been responsible for the roads of New Delhi built for the great Durbar of 1911.

The plan for the Imperial was like two Orthodox crosses superimposed on each other, allowing for twelve 90-degree corners on the exterior. The concrete façade was painted white and the windows were metal in the Art Deco style, but doorways were framed in red sandstone recalling the colour of many of Delhi's older buildings.

C.G. Blomfield and Mr Singh were to have plenty of dealings with Lady Willingdon, who took a keen interest in the interior finish of 'her' hotel. According to hotel legend, the stock of two Italian marble merchants was entirely depleted during the hotel's completion. Her Ladyship also decided on the name 'Imperial', a common one for hotels across Europe but with particular resonances given that India was called the jewel in the crown of the British Empire.

FREEMAN FREEMAN-THOMAS, 1ST MARQUESS OF WILLINGDON

Sadly, the Willingdons did not stay long enough in Delhi to enjoy its new hotel. On 18 April 1936 the Marquess's five-year term as Viceroy and Governor-General of India ended and he returned to the UK, where he became a favourite tennis partner of George V. While the Imperial is in many ways Lady Willingdon's memorial, it's worth noting that her husband is commemorated by the Willingdon Sports Club in Mumbai. The Viceroy established this club (with membership open to both Indians and British) after being denied entry to the Royal Bombay Yacht Club because he was in the company of Indian friends.

When the Imperial opened in 1936 it surprised people with its modernity and unusual floor plan, a sequence of Art Deco courtyards with low, wide corridors connecting them.

Twenty-four elegant king palm trees lined the road to the hotel's lofty *porte-cloche*. They still do today.

An unusual feature of the hotel was its ballroom, built not on the ground floor but on the first with terraces, accessed by French windows and extending over the verandas below. Today a photo is displayed in the ballroom showing the seated figures of Jawaharlal Nehru, Mahatma Gandhi, Muhammad Ali Jinnah and Lord Louis Mountbatten. This venue was chosen for independence discussions not just for its size, but because of its position upstairs facing onto open lawns. It was easy to keep secure – and it lent a certain dignity to some very important proceedings.

The hotel's bar is on the ground floor and called Patiala Peg. This commemorates the hugely wealthy Maharajah of Patiala. There is an old connection with the hotel here because in 1880 R.B.S. Narain Singh was awarded a lucrative contract by the then Maharajah to build part of the Patiala Tunnel in Punjab. It was the Maharajah's son, however, the handsome and extravagant Maharajah Bhupinder Singh (1891–1938) whose name is commemorated by this dark-panelled bar.

Fabulously wealthy, the young Maharajah was renowned for his prowess on the cricket pitch. He also maintained a polo team and a cricket team that were considered among the best in India. On one occasion he arranged a tent-pegging bout against an Irish regimental polo team. So worried was the Maharajah that his own team would lose, that he made sure the Irish visitors were given over-generous measures of alcohol the night before their encounter. The Patiala team duly triumphed and in their honour all measures in the new Patiala Peg bar are 75ml rather than standard 60ml.

The truth about the bars at the Imperial is much more interesting than the myth.

ASIA

THE ORIENTAL HOTEL, BANGKOK, THAILAND (1877)
MANDARIN ORIENTAL BANGKOK

The Oriental Hotel in Bangkok was originally just a few rooms and a lot of verandas on the banks of the busy Maenam river (Chao Phraya today). It was built in 1860 in response to the opening up of the Kingdom of Siam to western trade, following the 1855 Treaty of Friendship with Britain.

The owner of this 'boarding house for seafarers' was Captain James White. In 1863, after White's death by drowning in the Maenam river, the boarding house was taken over by two American businessmen who named it the Oriental. White's modest structure burned down two years later and another hotel briefly stood on this spot before in 1877 a brand-new enterprise was constructed by three Danish seamen called Andersen, Andersen, and Kinch. Their venture, a teak wood structure with a red tiled roof, quickly grew into the Oriental Hotel, Store and Chandlery.

By 1887 the Danes were employing a professional manager, George Troisoeufs, and a whole new wing had been added. This was a gracious two-storey building facing the river. It had been created in concrete but polished to resemble stone. The extension was said to be the most luxurious building outside Bangkok's palaces. It had mahogany furniture, wallpaper from Paris and broad carpeted verandas. Today it is the heart of the modern hotel complex and known as the Authors' Wing.

In December 1890 the hotel received a royal visitor. King Chulalongkorn was riding the tiger of modernisation in Siam while trying to stop Britain and France dismembering his kingdom. He wanted to inspect the Danish hotel downstream to see if it was suitable for an important guest who would be arriving in the new year, Crown Prince Nicholas of Russia. The king must have been impressed. The following year Chulalongkorn personally escorted the future Tsar and his entourage to the Oriental Hotel where they were introduced to the manager, Henry W. Smith, formerly of Astor House in Shanghai. Nicholas was installed in Bedroom No. 1 with its river view and blue drawing room. His officers proceeded to drink Mr Smith dry and he had difficulty replenishing his stock to keep up with them.

As was fashionable at the time, the hotel boasted an American Bar. Its counter was made of teak and marble. It had two pool tables and – unusually – displayed a portrait of George Washington.

In 1893 H.N. Andersen, the remaining Danish partner, sold the hotel to the American Franklin 'Bill' Hurst who had arrived with a railway survey team. The deal obliged Hurst to continue to buy hotel essentials like Krug champagne and Château Lafite-Rothschild through Andersen's East Asiatic Company.

In July that same year French warships anchored directly in front of the hotel with their guns aimed at the royal palace. In what was to become known as the Paknam Incident, a Siamese fort and some gunboats had fired on the French navy further down the river. Chulalongkorn did what he could to make peace. In the end that meant handing over Laos to France.

In the 1890s a stay at the Oriental was usually preceded by a river transfer via the hotel's steam launch which would meet the newly arrived ships. Edmund Chandler of the British *Daily Mail* wrote glowingly of reaching the Oriental and 'a soft bed, a European menu, and contact with one's fellow creatures'.

The lucrative hotel changed hands quite often. In 1904 it was forced to close down briefly because of debts run up by F.S. Robertson, the then owner, but by 1906 it was back in business under a new manager, Madame M.O. Bujault. Madame Bujault was one of three remarkable women who brought stability to the Oriental. She imported a Viennese orchestra and a chef from Paris, no mean feat but increasingly essential to maintaining an international clientele at the beginning of the twentieth century. Madame Bujault was succeeded in 1910 by Marie Maire. Madame Maire's husband Auguste was officially the proprietor, but it was she who procured a hotel automobile, landscaped the garden down to the river and added 'modern toilet fittings'. Not surprisingly, when Peter Carl Fabergé came to Bangkok in 1911 to popularise his remarkable jewellery, he stayed as a guest of Madame Maire. The new King Rama VI was one of those who commissioned work from Fabergé.

The First World War had little direct impact on the Oriental Hotel apart from the stranding of Russian dancer Vaslav Nijinsky in Bangkok in 1916. The enterprising Madame Maire turned his misfortune to her advantage and presented the first display of western ballet in Siam at the Oriental.

After the War to End All Wars, Marie Maire founded the Oriental Hotel Company, which allowed her to raise huge sums of capital to refurbish the hotel and add what became known as the 'Ambassador Wing'. By 1927 the Oriental boasted a grand French-style dining room, a bathroom attached to

every bedroom and electric lights throughout. The maximum number of guests was 50 and copious amounts of mosquito netting were provided for all. The writer and bon viveur Noël Coward and the Woolworth heiress Barbara Hutton stayed at the Oriental during the 1930s – at different times – confirming its status as the premier address in Siam.

SOMERSET MAUGHAM

One of those who stayed during the reign of Madame Maire was the British author W. Somerset Maugham, who wrote: 'My room faced the river. It was dark, one of a long line with a veranda on each side of it, the breeze blew through, but it was stifling.' Maugham soon fell ill, his temperature reaching 105. Having trained as a doctor he knew immediately it was malaria.

One day, lying feverish in his room, Maugham overheard Madame Maire telling the local doctor: 'I can't have him die here, you know. You must take him to hospital.'

The doctor suggested they gave it a day or two.

'Well don't leave it too long!'

He later put this alarming conversation into his book of travels, *The Gentleman in the Parlour* (1930).

In 1932 Madame Maire sold the Oriental and after the Japanese invasion of Thailand in 1941, the hotel was leased to the Japanese army as an officers' club, under the management of the Imperial Hotel in Tokyo. Unfortunately at the end of the war it was used to house liberated Allied prisoners of war, who – in the belief that it was a Japanese property – smashed up the building. The hotel was sold off for just $250 to a consortium of six people who included the American Jim Thompson, who was to revitalise the Thai silk industry in the 1950s, and Germaine Krull, a journalist and photographer from Germany. Although Krull had no hotel experience, she took over as manager and became the third remarkable woman to revitalise the Oriental. In 1958 the Oriental expanded again with a ten-storey Tower Wing behind the Author's Wing. This boasted an elevator and even a restaurant on the top floor, something of a novelty in Bangkok at the time.

In 1985 the Oriental Hotel, now part of the Italthai company, joined its name with another hotel in the same group, the Mandarin in Hong Kong, to form the Mandarin Oriental. The rest, as they say, is hotel history.

THE CONTINENTAL HOTEL, SAIGON, VIETNAM (1880)
HOTEL CONTINENTAL SAIGON, HO CHI MINH CITY

The Continental was constructed in 1878 by Pierre Cazeau, a manufacturer of domestic appliances in French Indochina. It opened in 1880 and was from its inception a French hotel aimed at the French traveller.

Its location on Rue Catinat was perfect, being at the midpoint between Notre Dame cathedral, the post office, the port and Hôtel de Ville (now the People's Community Office of Hồ Chí Minh City). In 1911 a Théâtre Municipal was opened in the square in front of the hotel, making the Continental the hotel of choice in this Vietnamese mini-

Photo: Franklin Heijnen

Paris. 'Les broussailleux' (Frenchmen living outside Saigon) stayed here when attending the opera. They could sit outside the hotel on its broad *terrasse* and imagine they were back in France. There were a number places to stay in Saigon but only one of them was referred to simply as 'the hotel'.

The Continental also attracted travelling aristocrats and colonial adventurers, one of the most celebrated being Marie-Charles David de Mayréna, an eccentric Frenchman who visited in 1888. Among his adventures, Mayréna managed to get locals to declare him King of the Sedang (the northern Central Highlands of Vietnam) before dying in 1890.

The author and journalist André Malraux stayed at the Continental in the 1920s when he was setting up his anti-colonial newspaper *Indochine*. In his *Antimémoires*, Malraux wrote of *l'heure verte*: 'the green hour on the Continental terrace when short evenings used to fall on carob trees and the sound of bells could be heard as coaches crossed Rue Catinat.'

In 1922, reporting for his paper *L'Excelsior*, journalist Albert Londres wrote with amusement about two 'heroic' guests who braved the heat of Saigon every evening on the terrasse of the Continental dressed in smoking jackets and high collars.

In 1892 the Continental was bought by restaurateur Charles Grosstephan, and then by Prince Ferdinand, Duc de Montpensier, as an investment in 1911. It subsequently passed through a number of hands before finding its last private owner. In 1930, Mathieu Francini, a Corsican whom some labelled a gangster, bought the Continental and set out to make it more Parisian than anything in Paris. 'There had to be gaiety and *chic*,' wrote the owner's son. At this time the Continental became a byword for sophisticated entertainment and covert affairs between European men and local women.

Noël Coward visited in the 1930s, having driven down from Hanoi and – so he declared – composing *Mad Dogs and Englishmen* while on the road. Coward recalled that from the terrasse he could watch 'the beau monde bouncing up and down the Rue Catinat in rickshaws'. He also recalled how the hotel orchestra played 'selections from *Tosca*, *Madame Butterfly* and the tinkling French operettas of the nineties every evening'.

HORACE BLEAKLEY

The British also visited, among them Horace Bleakley (1868–1931), celebrated author of *The Hangmen of England: How They Hanged and Whom They Hanged*. In his Asian travelogue he recorded: 'the scene is reminiscent of a restaurant in the Champs Elysées. Across the road a smartly dressed crowd emerges from the vestibule of the principal cinema theatre at frequent intervals during the performance and joins the symposium gathered at little tables on the pavement in front of the hotel. A stream of cars and rickshaws, filled with lightly clad men and women come to take air, glides incessantly along the street. A dance, perhaps, is in progress in the lounge of the hotel, facing the square.'

The Continental continued as a sound, slightly racy investment until the beginning of what became known in Vietnam as 'the American War'. In 1954 the French army was defeated at Dien Bien Phu and Saigon began to fill up with American 'advisors'. From 1952 Graham Greene was at the hotel, in Room 214. In between reporting on the fighting for *The Times* and *Le Figaro*, he constructed a prescient novel about the coming disastrous colonial war: *The Quiet American*. Not only was the book written at the Continental, much of its action took place in and around the hotel.

Saigon was transformed by the American War and not in a pleasant way. Nicknamed Honda City, the capital became a place of bars, drugs and open prostitution. The opera house served as the National Assembly building and the Continental was transformed too, as its famous terrasse was deemed unsafe. The legendary US reporter Walter Cronkite was one of many who moved to drinking in the first-floor bar overlooking the inner courtyard which journalists nicknamed 'The Continental Shelf'. Among war correspondents it was believed they were safe on 'The Shelf' from any grenades tossed into the hotel.

In 1975 Viet Cong forces took Saigon and Philippe Francini, son of Matthieu, had to surrender ownership of the Continental, which became the property of the Socialist Republic of Vietnam and was renamed the 'Dong Khoi' (Simultaneous Uprising). In 2002, after a thaw in US relations, it was used extensively in the second film of *The Quiet American*, starring Michael Caine and Brendan Fraser.

Today the hotel has reverted to its original name and stands as a remarkable period piece amid all the high-rise Park Hyatts, Sofitels and Novotels of modern capitalism.

RAFFLES HOTEL, SINGAPORE (1887)

In December 1887 the four splendidly moustachioed Sarkies brothers from Armenia, proprietors of the Eastern and Oriental Hotel in Penang, opened a new venture in Singapore. Rather than name it after a particular clientele – as was common at the time – they adopted the name of the colony's founder, Sir Stamford Raffles (1781–1826).

The building chosen for this development was a pre-existing 1830s beach bungalow on the south side of the island. In 1878 it had been converted into a hotel by Dr Charles Emerson but on his death in 1883, the ambitious Sarkies stepped in. Their new hotel had ten rooms and its proximity to the Singapore Strait promised fresh air. Singapore was a busy trading port in the 1890s and within a few years the brothers had added a pair of two-storey wings with 22 bedrooms in each.

In 1892, with the oldest brother Martin in retirement, and Aviet and Arshak managing their hotel in Penang, Tigran Sarkies was left in charge of Raffles. In 1894, with an eye to expansion, he opened a Palm Court Wing in a building next to the hotel which the Sarkies had leased. By 1899 the original core of the hotel had been rebuilt to designs by R.A.J. Bidwell of Swan and Maclaren, Singapore. Here finally arose the building we know today. Within just twelve years an elegant three-storey Neo-Renaissance palazzo with 100 bedrooms and terracotta roof tiles had replaced the old twin-winged bungalow. The hotel advertised that it was the first in Singapore to use electric lighting and to employ a French chef. Electric fans were also installed, but there was local opposition to this innovation so Tigran Sarkies had to agree that punkah wallahs who worked the manual fans could stay on.

LITERARY RAFFLES

Novelist Joseph Conrad is believed to have been one of Raffles Hotel's earliest guests during his seafaring days. Not long after, the young Rudyard Kipling dined at Raffles and wrote that 'the food is as excellent as the rooms are bad. Let the traveller take note. Feed at Raffles and sleep at Hotel de l'Europe.' This recommendation of a hated rival did not go down well at Raffles.

In 1921 W. Somerset Maugham made the first of a number of visits to Raffles and in 1930 the writer and actor Noël Coward arrived. He was playing the part of Captain Stanhope in the First World War drama *Journey's End*, which was touring the Far East.

All three authors were said to have drunk at the hotel's famous Long Bar, which in the 1920s was located in the lobby, snaking for twenty metres between pillars that supported the first floor.

By 1920 local newspapers were declaring Raffles Hotel 'the most magnificent establishment of its kind East of Suez' with 'the finest ballroom in the East'. Its bar and billiard room had been enlarged to hold six tables, and legendary bartender Ngiam Tong Boon had created the Million Dollar Cocktail and the Singapore Sling.

In the 1920s Arshak, the youngest of the four brothers, was causing concern at the Eastern and Oriental in Penang by dint of his generous, even extravagant, behaviour, but the Sarkies' financial problems would not come to the fore until the Great Depression of the 1930s. For the moment in the 1920s things could not be better in Singapore. A 'Raffles March' dedicated to Tigran Sarkies was composed. The hotel's runners were sent to every newly arrived ship to help visitors disembark (and subtly tout for trade) and rickshaw drivers were well-paid to divert the newly arrived away from Hôtel de L'Europe, Raffles' only serious rival. The Sarkies' hotel was so keen to exceed all others that it even offered guests its own darkroom and telegraph office. Not surprisingly, the usual globe-hopping celebrities arrived while passing through Singapore, including Charlie Chaplin, Maurice Chevalier, and Jean Harlow. Decorum at Raffles was strictly if subtly enforced. Any man who tried to take a local woman to dinner at Raffles would be left in no doubt his behaviour was *infra dig*, and any man who took to the dance floor without his dinner jacket would find that the orchestra stopped playing until he left.

In 1931 the Great Depression caught up with Singapore following a slump in the Malayan rubber trade. That year Arshak Sarkies, the last surviving of the four brothers, died and both Raffles and the Eastern and Oriental in Penang went into receivership. Two years later a new public company called Raffles Hotel Ltd was formed with Teddy Troller, yet another formidable Swiss hotelier, as general manager. Raffles' recovery was slow but it received a boost in 1933 when its long-term rival, Hôtel de L'Europe, succumbed to financial pressures and closed. Now there was only one first-class hotel on Singapore, and by 1934 Raffles had expanded to 120 rooms.

On 7 December 1941 Imperial Japanese forces unexpect-edly attacked Singapore, Hong Kong and the United States

and many British families fled down the Malayan Peninsula with the Japanese army in pursuit. They congregated at Raffles Hotel where the colonial ethos was reassuring, but the Japanese captured an RAF airfield, dropped bombs on the city and beat back the British army until on 15 February 1942 it surrendered. A story runs that the first Japanese soldiers reaching the Raffles Hotel found the British waltzing. Couples then defiantly serenaded the invaders with 'There'll Always be an England'.

Terrible years followed on Singapore, for prisoners of war and civilians alike. Raffles was requisitioned as a *ryokan* (traditional inn) and renamed Syonan. The name Syonan meant 'Light of the South', Japan's name for their new conquest. The hotel's silver had already been buried under the floor of the Palm Court and would not re-emerge until 1945 when Japan surrendered Singapore to Admiral Lord Louis Mountbatten. On the night of 22 August that year 300 Japanese officers held a farewell party at the hotel, drinking sake before committing ritual suicide.

In the months that followed the Raffles Hotel became a temporary transit camp for POWs released under the military administration – and was judged to be in a poor condition. Reconstruction began and by 1953 Raffles Hotel Ltd was able to reopen its grill room as the Elizabethan in honour of the coronation of Queen Elizabeth II. A new generation of stars – including the nomadic Ava Gardner and glittering Elizabeth Taylor – visited. Raffles also featured in the 1967 film *Pretty Polly*, based on a Singaporean short story written by Noël Coward and featuring Trevor Howard and Hayley Mills.

In 1987 the Singapore government rightly designated Raffles a National Monument and in 1989 the hotel embarked on a two-and-a-half-year refurbishment that aimed to recreate the ambience of Raffles in the 1920s. The famous

Long Bar was relocated up a flight of steps to its own room of wicker chairs and traditional reed fans, with a polished teakwood bar and monkey nuts. For decades boxes of monkey nuts were placed on tables and customers were encouraged to drop the casings on the floor and crush them underfoot to feed the wooden boards. It's as much a Raffles tradition as the Singapore Sling and definitely set to continue.

GRAND HÔTEL MÉTROPOLE PALACE, HANOI, VIETNAM (1901)
SOFITEL LEGEND MÉTROPOLE HANOI

Most grand hotels tend to settle down to a comfortable middle age. Usually it is in the struggle to create the hotel that all the dramas occur. Not so for Hôtel Métropole in Hanoi, but then this was always an unusual project. It was founded by one of the most unlikely hotel entrepreneurs: Gustave-Émile Dumoutier (1850–1904), the son of a wealthy French industrialist who studied at the Sorbonne and developed a passion for Asian antiquities.

Graduating from the School of Oriental Languages in Paris, Dumoutier travelled to French Indochina in 1886 with the brilliant physiologist and left-wing politician Paul Bert. The two men lived in the French protectorate of Tonkin where Dumoutier was made chief education officer and Bert was appointed resident-general.

Despite the dangers inherent in going up-country, Dumoutier carried out excavations in the pirate-ridden Red River Delta and explored the Black River. After the sudden death of Bert from dysentery in November 1886,

Photo: Daaé

Dumoutier stayed on in Tonkin and was put in charge of organising the Annamite Pavilion at the World Fair in Paris for 1889. He also carried out scientific explorations in Canton, Macao, Hong Kong, Shanghai and Peking, and visited the Great Wall.

Then in 1899 Dumoutier branched out in a very different direction, filing a request to convert the houses he had bought on a lakeside in Hanoi into a hotel. The capital for this venture (500,000 francs) was provided by a local French businessman called André Ducamp. Two years later in 1901 the Grand Hôtel Métropole Palace was opened. It was a remarkably imposing building for its time, considering that Hanoi was such a swampy backwater.

Ducamp's money was well spent. Behind a white Neoclassical façade graced with green shutters, the hotel was wood-panelled throughout. Its ground floor was protected from the sun by the overhanging wrought-iron balconies of the first and second floors, and the whole structure was dominated by a Belle Époque dome. The main façade spanned over 80 metres. It was simply the largest hotel in Indochina at that time. In March 1901 *La Revue indochinoise* of Hanoi referred to it admiringly as 'un immense hôtel'.

The new hotel was operated by Compagnie Française Immobilière, who also provided the restaurant cars on trains between Hanoi and the cities of the south. Ducamp would be general manager for decades but Dumoutier soon retired. In 1903 he donated his collections to the École française d'Extrême-Orient in Paris and died a year later, leaving behind him numerous archaeological studies, the first school textbooks published in Indochina, and a very splendid hotel.

Whether Dumoutier's business venture was anything more than a money-making scheme with a view towards his retirement or an investment in the city he loved is unclear.

Regardless of the motivation, founding a large hotel in Hanoi proved a shrewd business move. In 1902 the French moved the capital of Indochina from Saigon to Hanoi. The city's population of Europeans now swelled to 3,000 and they and their visitors needed a grand hotel.

ALFRED CUNNINGHAM

An early visitor to Hôtel Métropole was the Hong Kong-based American journalist Alfred Cunningham who in 1902 travelled extensively with his camera for a book entitled *The French in Tonkin and South China*, in which he wrote:

'The most important hotel in Hanoi is the Hôtel Métropole. It is a splendid building, only very recently erected, and is situated on the boulevard Henri-Rivière, immediately opposite the Résidence Supérieure. The hotel is elegantly furnished, each bedroom has a bathroom and there is a public hall, salon de conversation, reading room. The sanitary arrangements are perfect, and the general accommodation leaves nothing to be desired.'

The First World War depleted Indochina of its travellers and much of its population. Fifty thousand soldiers and 49,000 workers were drafted from Vietnamese villages to serve on the French battlefront. The party continued at the Métropole, however. The first silent movies ever shown in what is now called Vietnam were presented at the hotel in 1916.

The success of the Métropole under its remaining owner André Ducamp is reflected in his being made vice president of the Hanoi Chamber of Commerce as well as vice president of Hanoi Trade Fair Managing Committee in 1925. Another accolade came in 1936 when Charlie Chaplin and Paulette Goddard spent their honeymoon at the Métropole after secretly marrying in Shanghai.

In 1940 the French colonial authorities, loyal to the Vichy regime, acquiesced to a takeover of Indochina by the Imperial Japanese army. The following year Hồ Chí Minh returned from exile to form the Việt Minh who would fight both the Japanese and French – and later the Americans – for the return of their country.

In 1945 when the Japanese army withdrew, France attempted to reassert its authority over Indochina but in August a Vietnamese insurrection began under Hồ. The following month Chinese troops arrived in Hanoi to support the new Democratic Republic of Vietnam. The French population of Hanoi began to leave and in 1946 the last French owners of the Métropole sold the hotel to a Chinese businessman. Eight years later in August 1954, after the partition of Vietnam north and south, it was nationalised. The Métropole now became a government rest house for VIPs and was renamed, tellingly, Thong Nhat Hotel (Reunification Hotel).

In 1960 Hồ, now president of the Democratic Republic of Vietnam, visited the hotel. In 1962 a third floor was added, removing that very French-looking dome. Meanwhile the escalation of the Vietnam War following a full scale commitment of American forces led to the building of an underground bomb shelter. It was dug into the courtyard of the hotel with a concrete ceiling one metre thick. The shelter could accommodate guests, but the hotel staff were expected to stay outside defending the hotel against looters with their rifles while fifteen of their number manned an anti-aircraft gun mounted on the new flat roof.

During Vietnam's 'American War' the Métropole was renowned as the only hotel with sufficient protection for its VIPs. In 1971 the Hollywood actress Jane Fonda was a guest for two months in a room on the second floor while protesting against American involvement in Vietnam. In December 1972 the American songwriter and activist Joan Baez sheltered at the Métropole during the eleven-day-long Christmas bombing campaign over Hanoi and sang to her companions inside the bunker.

In April 1975, troops of the North Vietnamese Army entered Saigon, the capital of South Vietnam, and the American War came to an end. By this time, like most buildings in Hanoi, the Thong Nhat Hotel needed major refurbishment. It finally received it in 1987 when the French Pullman hotel chain entered into a joint venture with the Vietnamese government to restore the hotel. Returned to its original name of Métropole, the hotel was completely rebuilt and reopened in March 1992.

In 2012 a new tourist attraction in Hanoi came into existence when the old air raid shelter was rediscovered and opened up to the public. It's hardly the kind of facility that Gustave-Émile Dumoutier had in mind in 1901, but nothing that brings in tourists can ever be entirely bad.

THE CATHAY HOTEL, SHANGHAI, CHINA (1928)
FAIRMONT PEACE HOTEL, SHANGHAI

The most famous hotel on Shanghai's Bund was originally intended as offices. The builder was Sir Victor Sassoon, the Harrow- and Cambridge-educated scion of a Baghdadi

Jewish family which had made its fortune in the nineteenth-century cotton and opium trades.

VICTOR SASSOON

Victor Sassoon served in the Royal Flying Corps in the First World War. In 1916, at the age of 34, he survived a plane crash that damaged his legs but that did not diminish his energy for hard work and fun. When his father died in 1924, Sassoon became 3rd Baronet of Bombay. He moved to India, where he managed his family's textile mills and served in the Legislative Assembly. In the 1920s and 30s, he transferred much of the family wealth to Shanghai, helping fuel the property boom along the Bund. At one point Sassoon owned over 1,800 buildings in Shanghai, including the Metropole Hotel, also designed by Palmer and Turner (see page 274).

Sassoon always walked with two silver-topped canes to cope with his war injuries but made light of his disability. With the coming of Communism he packed a single suitcase and quietly boarded a boat out of Shanghai. 'I gave up on India – and China gave me up,' he remarked.

Sassoon lived out the rest of his days in the Bahamas with his nurse 'Barnsie', whom he eventually married. Photos in the hotel's Peace Gallery show him looking tanned and jovial at the end of his life. After his death in 1961 Lady Sassoon continued to host her husband's black-tie Heart Ball each year over the Valentine's Day weekend to raise money for Bahamian orphans.

In 1926 Sassoon commissioned plans for what would become the Cathay Hotel. The location was a lucrative one. At the intersection of the Bund and East Nanjing Road, this new skyscraper would face both the Huangpu River and the largest shopping street in Asia.

British architect George Leopold Wilson (1880–1967), who ran the Shanghai branch of Palmer and Turner, a leading Hong Kong architectural firm, drew up plans for the tallest and most sophisticated office building in China. There were structural problems given that the river had laid down hundreds of metres of soft alluvium over the past millennia. Since 1910 architects had been using concrete rafts on which to 'float' their buildings along the Bund, but the raft supporting Sassoon House was the largest yet, 99 metres by 57 metres and pinned through the ground by a thousand pine pilings.

Halfway through construction, the energetic Sassoon decided that his 83-metre skyscraper would become a hotel. The ground floor would still be given over to shops and banks and the floors above to offices, but at the fourth floor the hotel's bedrooms would begin and the eighth floor was to be both reception and the hotel ballroom (as today). Above that was the Tower Restaurant where a young Christopher Isherwood would one day gossip with Freddy Kaufmann, the restaurant manager, after saying goodbye to Berlin. Above the restaurant, at the base of the distinctive green copper pyramidical roof, was to be Sir Victor's private apartment and dining room where he could entertain celebrity guests, of which there were many.

In the bedrooms below, guests enjoyed solid marble baths filled with spring water from silver taps. Individual rooms were decorated in a range of styles that included Jacobean, Georgian, Indian, Chinese, Japanese, and Art Deco. The

Photo: Adrian Mourby

newly named Cathay Hotel marked a shift in the design of Shanghai's Bund. After its opening in 1928 the city turned its back on the staid Neo-Renaissance style of granite architecture that made every building look like a bank.

Once the public were admitted, the architects were criticised for having ignored *feng shui* by having a front door opening on to running water, so a second entrance was opened up on Nanjing Road. The two entrances converged on an octagon that is still a feature of the hotel today.

Victor Sassoon threw the most lavish Jazz Age parties in his ballroom (now known as the Peace Hall), with its priceless Lalique Corridor of pioneering glasswork by the exclusive Paris company. At one event, Sassoon appeared as the ringmaster for a circus-themed fancy dress evening. Though barred from membership of the Shanghai Club because he was Jewish, Sassoon's invitations were, ironically, much sought-after by the club's all-English committee. The affable Victor said the paradox amused him.

On the ground floor, not far from the Octagon, Sassoon also built an English pub with faux wooden rafters and half-timbered panelling which he named the Fox and Hound. However, once word got around that some of Shanghai's best jazz was played in the hotel, it became known as the Jazz Bar.

In the 1930s many refugees and travellers came to Shanghai to live and work. Among these self-styled 'Shanghailanders' were almost 20,000 White Russians and Russian Jews. By 1932, Shanghai had become the world's fifth largest city with a population of 70,000 foreigners. It was also known as 'The Paris of the East, the New York of the West'. This golden age for expats ended in 1941 when the Imperial Japanese army invaded Shanghai's foreign concessions, and hotels and offices along the Bund were occupied. Sir Victor did what he could to help the large Jewish community but these were very bad times in Shanghai.

In 1948, seeing that Mao's communists were winning the Chinese Civil War, Sir Victor slipped away from Shanghai and relocated to Nassau in the Bahamas, and in 1949 he sold all his business interests in China. The old Cathay Hotel was nationalised and turned into government offices. In 1952 it was reopened as a hotel and in 1956 it was renamed the Peace Hotel by the somewhat belligerent Chinese government. During the Cultural Revolution (1966–76) the hotel was used by the Gang of Four, particularly by Zhang Chunqiao, who advocated dictatorship over the bourgeoisie as he commanded Shanghai's commune from luxurious quarters in the Peace Hotel.

After the opening up of the Chinese state in the 1980s, following Deng Xiaoping's declaration that to get rich is glorious, the Peace Hotel was restored to its former Art Deco glory at a cost of   US$41 million. The Canadian hotel giant Fairmont was brought in to manage it. The Old Peace Hotel Band, which had been disbanded under Communism, reformed in the Fox and Hound. Even though they were mostly in their 90s they undertook to play every evening at 6.30.

Sir Victor would definitely have applauded.

THE PENINSULA, HONG KONG, CHINA (1928)

Baghdad is the surprise connection between the Peninsula in Hong Kong and that other great palace of 1920s hospitality, the Peace Hotel in Shanghai. The builder of the Peace Hotel was Sir Victor Sassoon, great-grandson of David Sassoon

(1792–1864), a Baghdadi Jew who moved to Bombay and set up a very lucrative trade in cotton and opium.

David Sassoon had a policy of employing other Baghdadi Jews, including the Kadoorie family who eventually represented him in Shanghai. The Kadoories soon went into business on their own in Shanghai and Hong Kong. In the 1920s two of their number, the brothers Elias and Eleazer Kadoorie, decided to found 'the finest hotel east of Suez' in Hong Kong.

Sir Elias Kadoorie died in 1922 before the mighty Peninsula opened, so his younger brother, Sir Eleazer (known as Elly), saw the hotel through to its (much delayed) opening in December 1928. The building was a sturdy Neoclassical New York style of hotel and its location in Kowloon was perfect. It stood close to the railway station and directly opposite the quayside where ocean liner passengers disembarked.

Hong Kong was at this time leased to the British on a 99-year lease and had become a major *entrepôt* thanks to its free port status. Prosperity attracted migrants from Europe and Asia and by 1925 – the year the Peninsula should have opened – its population was nearly three-quarters of a million. The governor in 1925, Cecil Clementi, was fluent in Cantonese and ran the Crown Colony without a translator. This was a golden city for Europeans whose wealthy lifestyle was captured by Somerset Maugham in his novel *The Painted Veil*.

When Hong Kong's splendid new six-storey hotel opened, it was to music from the band of the 2nd Battalion the King's Own Scottish Borderers. The massive lobby (7,500 sq ft) was decorated in Italian Cinquecento style. From the lobby two wings ran off on either side, creating an open-ended courtyard in which taxis and rickshaws could turn. At first-floor level there was a veranda on the three sides of the courtyard with views of the railway station and harbour beyond, but it was the views inside that captivated visitors. There was a Moorish Bar, a blue-domed banqueting hall, a marble tea lounge, and a children's dining room. There was also a barber shop and what is now one of the oldest fashion arcades in Hong Kong.

Reports of the opulence of the Peninsula soon spread its reputation around the world. Its unrivalled status in Hong Kong was confirmed in 1936 when the most famous film star of his day, Charlie Chaplin, arrived by ship to promote his film *Modern Times* – and took a suite at the Peninsula.

But this heyday was to be short-lived. By 1938 Hong Kong was effectively surrounded by forces of the Imperial Japanese army who had been fighting their way through China. On 8 December 1941, just eight hours after the aerial attack on Pearl Harbor, the Japanese 23rd Army and Air Unit, as well as the 2nd China Expeditionary Fleet, attacked Hong Kong. With virtually no air defence, the Hong Kong garrison was defeated in two weeks. On Christmas Day 1941 Sir Mark Aitchison Young, the governor of the island who had only been in post for two months, surrendered in person to General Takashi Sakai at the army's new headquarters on the third floor of the Peninsula Hotel. The Governor was confined for two months in one of the hotel suites before he was shipped to a prison in Shanghai. The Peninsula itself was renamed the 'Toa Hotel' (East Asia Hotel), with all rooms reserved for Japanese officers and visiting dignitaries.

Very dark days ensued in Hong Kong, with the local population treated even worse than the Europeans. In 1942, Sir Elly Kadoorie was taken from his home in Shanghai and interned in a Japanese prison camp for foreign civilians where he died in 1944.

Photo: Andrew Martin

A HOTEL AT WAR

In October 1942 Colonel Robert Lee Scott, Jr of the USAAF led an attack on Japanese shipping anchored in Hong Kong harbour and broke off to attack the Peninsula Hotel on his own:

'So I looped above Victoria Harbor and dove for the Peninsula Hotel. My tracers ripped into the shining plate glass of the penthouses on its top, and I saw the broken windows cascade like snow to the streets, many floors below. I laughed, for I knew that behind those windows were Japanese high officers, enjoying that modern hotel. When I got closer I could see uniformed figures going down the fire escapes, and I shot at them ... I turned for one more run on the packed fire escapes filled with Jap soldiers, but my next burst ended very suddenly. I was out of ammunition.'

From *God is my Co-Pilot* by Robert Lee Scott

On 14 August 1945 Japan surrendered following the atom-bomb blasts over Hiroshima and Nagasaki, and in May 1946 Mark Aitchison Young returned to Hong Kong as governor as the process of reconstruction began.

The years after the Second World War were ones of increasing success for the Peninsula. In 1953 it opened Gaddi's, the first fine dining restaurant serving French cuisine in the Far East. Sir Horace Kadoorie, son of Sir Elly, named it after the hotel's general manager, Leo Gaddi (in office 1948–60). His rationale was that Gaddi would never let standards slip anywhere that bore his name.

A glamorous but not entirely surprising roster of Hollywood stars came to stay: Elizabeth Taylor, Peter O'Toole, Kirk Douglas, Douglas Fairbanks Jr, and Shirley MacLaine, who one evening in 1972 objected to the size of her dinner bill. When *maître d'* Ricky Vaterlaus explained that he had added the cost of the silver chopstick holders that had gone missing from her table, she laughed and tipped out her handbag, showing they were indeed inside.

In 1994 a truly massive extension to the hotel was added in the form of a 30-storey tower in matching style, which was topped off by a helipad for private transfers from the airport. Underneath the helipad sat the Felix Bar which was named after another legendary general manager of the Peninsula, Felix Bieger (in office 1970–94). The Felix not only has a superb view of the nightly light show over Hong Kong's harbour, but has probably the most dramatic vista in the world from its urinals.

In 1999 Hong Kong was returned to China as a Special Administrative Region of the People's Republic but this did not dampen the spirits of those running the Peninsula. In 2006, in keeping with the sheer stylish extravagance of the hotel, fourteen Rolls-Royce Phantoms painted in the hotel's signature green were purchased to replace the ageing fleet of Rolls-Royce Silver Spurs. This was the largest single order ever placed with the British Rolls-Royce company.

The hotel today is the flagship property of the Peninsula Hotels group headed by Sir Michael Kadoorie, grandson of Sir Elly Kadoorie and the sixth wealthiest person in Hong Kong. Far from resting on their laurels, the group is currently opening Peninsula hotels all around the world, proof that the grand hotel is not just alive in the twenty-first century – it is thriving as never before.

AFTERWORDS

A PERSONAL NOTE

My mother, Peggy Mourby always loved hotels. As a girl she used to stay in London with her favourite aunt (known, uniquely among the family aunts as 'Auntie' with no Christian name attached). They would have tea at some of London's grandest hotels, and Auntie would always say, 'Aren't we out?'

Being 'out' in the 1930s meant experiencing the very best hospitality in the capital.

My own childhood was less glamorous. I believe I was eight before I even stayed in a hotel. Up until then family holidays were spent in caravans (in effect camping in a harsh, ugly metal tent on two fixed wheels) or in boarding houses (living in someone's spare room with the obligation to be outside pacing the Promenade between certain hours and eating a set dinner when the landlady told you it was ready).

The first hotel I stayed at was on 'The Front' at Aberystwyth. For my English mother and Welsh schoolmaster father this was la dolce vita indeed. We could come and go as we pleased. We ate when we wanted to eat. We had the luxury of being right by the sea without the misery of spending days sitting on uncomfortable banquettes inside a tacky metal box while rain hammered insanely on the roof.

Every morning my father, in his blazer, would knock on the door of the bedroom I was sharing with my grandmother and he and I would go down to the rock pools and harvest whelks and limpets and other molluscs under the pier. Then we would take them back in my plastic bucket for Josefina, the hotel's Spanish cook-cum-waitress, to prepare for that evening.

What I loved about that week by the sea was not the foraged seafood – that would take at least another two decades – nor the décor – my mother was much more stylish – but the way this became our temporary home. We were welcome to come and go as we wished and whenever we came home Josefina was pleased to see us and keen to serve us.

When we left I cried (I did rather a lot of that in my first eleven years of life). Then I went to a school where I learned that boys did not cry and so I did not cry again until I discovered opera in my twenties. Reviewing opera across Europe and into Asia I stayed at many wonderful hotels, and the best of them transformed my view of the world. In these great theatres of hospitality I felt immediately at home.

I have never cried since when leaving a hotel, but that is because I know they will always be there and I can always go back. At the age of eight I feared I'd never be as happy again. That tall, narrow hotel in Aberystwyth – with its embossed wallpaper, over-the-top carpets and benign service – was my first hint that such a wonderful world existed. Since then I have visited lots of grand hotels and I have met owners and general managers who share my passion – because a truly grand hotel is about passion. For the staff it is a passion to give the guest whatever he or she wants and even exceed expectations. For the guest it is a passion to return.

In discovering the grand hotels of the world I finally discovered what that lovely narrow, slightly decrepit hotel in Aberystwyth was telling me all those years ago: here is a world where you are always welcome and where the staff make their arrangements around you, rather than you around them.

This book is about these wonderful hotels and the remarkable people who made them, and all their stories. A grand hotel is not about size or cost or grandeur but about a vision of making the needs of the customer paramount. It is also about love, or at least the simulacrum. A truly grand hotel makes us feel like we are loved, a cherished member of a great family, which explains why one can sometimes feel terribly cast out when leaving.

I got a taste of that in the 1960s and losing it has sent me all around the world ever since.

ACKNOWLEDGEMENTS

I am aware in writing this book that I'm building on the work of other hotel historians. In particular Andreas Augustin, President of Famous Hotels, who published or republished many of my early articles on hotels around the world. Andreas set a very high standard with his own hotel books, demonstrating that this delightful subject is also one that can be taken seriously.

I must also thank my wife, Kate, who not only gave invaluable advice on the first draft of this book but also joined me on many of the research trips. Travelling the world would not have been the same without her. Many travel writers – Somerset Maugham and Bruce Chatwin are particular examples – excised their companion from accounts they published of their 'lone' travels but anyone who travels a lot knows the companion is an invaluable asset.

I've also been greatly helped by British Airways, Virgin Airlines and easyJet, and in particular by Railbookers, whose help getting me around Europe has been invaluable.

The staff of all but one of the hotels featured in this book have been very helpful, but in addition to blanket thanks I'd like to single out the following: Maria Speridakos of Massachusetts Office of Travel and Tourism, Christine Rigamer of Gambel Communications in New Orleans, Nim Singh of the Canadian Tourist Commission in London, Nicholas Sciammarella at the Algonquin, Ariana Swedin and Suela Kacani at the Plaza, Philippe Parodi at the Biltmore and Suzie Sponder, Media Director for the Miami Visitor Bureau. Special thanks go to the Belmond team who arranged so much travel for me in the days of Orient Express and to Mirjam Peternek of Lemongrass PR who arranged my visit to Hawaii. In Britain thanks are due to Aysem Monaco-Imison of the Langham Hotel London, Michael Grange of the Macdonald Randolph in Oxford, Emma Allam of the Savoy, and Susan Scott, the Savoy's very fortunate archivist. Thanks also to Dale MacPhee of the Caledonian in Edinburgh, Georgina Bissenden at the Waldorf, London, Rosanna Fishbourne and her team at the Dorchester, and to Mark Needham and Brian Jenkins at the Midland, Morecambe.

In France Pauline Thomann at Le Meurice and Sofia Vandaele at the Hilton Paris Opera were very welcoming. Sabina Held at the Adlon Kempinski, Bettina Jamy-Stowasser and Helena Hartlauer of WienTourismus were also excellent hosts. Sandra Artacker at Hotel Sacher Wien answered lots of questions and even sent me a Sachertorte for research purposes. Pascal Buchs and Lucie Gerber at Geneva Tourism were very helpful, as were Pedro Deakin and Fabrice Thome at Four Seasons Hotel des Bergues and Sara Roloff's team at Switzerland Tourism.

I shared a great evening with Maximilien Haus at Baur au Lac and several with Thierry and Andrea Scherz in Gstaad. Maria Pajares and her team at Mason Rose were just wonderful, as were Rosie O'Brien and her colleagues at Rocco Forte. In Italy my special thanks to Fabiola Balduzzi in Rome, Cyndy Cruikshank and Eva Reidt of Starwood in Venice, Alain Bullo and Stefania Vaccari at the Londra Palace, Elena Scarpa of Hotel Sant Antonin, Venice, Riccardo Santi of the Grand Hôtel et de Milan, Valentina and Elena de Santis of Grand Hotel Tremezzo and finally Laura di Bert and the wonderful Walter Bolzonella of the Cipriani in Venice, creator of possibly the best martinis in the world.

Tim Ananiadis and Christine Papathanassiou of Hôtel Grande Bretagne, Athens were also very helpful and welcoming as were Magdalena Adamus at what used to be Le Meridien Bristol, Warsaw, Irina Khlopova at what is now the Belmond Grand Hotel Europe and Anna Kagan at the Astoria, St Petersburg. Thanks too to Ceyda Pekenc and Hulya Soylu of Redmint Communications, Tolga Tuyluoglu of Go Turkey, Sonam Shah of Brandman PR, Aparupa Ray Ganguly and Rucji Jain of the Imperial, Delhi, Nisha Dhage of Taj Hotels, Jessica Staley of Ann Scott PR, Karn Puntuhong of the Mandarin Oriental, Bangkok and Jessica Zhang of Fairmont Peace Hotel, Shanghai.

GUEST LIST

An index of famous people who have stayed at grand hotels

Abbas II, Khedive of Egypt 134

Abbot and Costello 92

Albert Victor, Prince of Wales 222

Alexander, Prince of Yugoslavia 231

Al-Fayed, Mohamed and Dodi 112

Alfonso XIII, King of Spain 99, 153, 178

Allégret, Yves 235

Allen, Woody 40, 97, 166

Amelia, Queen of Portugal 178

Amis, Kingsley and Hilly 68

Anderson, Sherwood 26

Armstrong, Louis 156

Ascencios, Natalie 37

Astor, John Jacob IV 82, 242

Astor, William Waldorf 79, 82

Atatürk, Mustapha Kemal, 193, 215–17

Auer, Leopold 199

Baedeker, Karl 221

Baez, Joan 272

Baker, Josephine 11, 13, 40, 126, 176, 234

Balfour, Arthur 110

Balmain, Pierre 236

Bankhead, Tallulah 37

Barry, Philip 35

Barrymore, John 36

Batista, Fulgencio, President of Cuba 231

Baxter, Anne 32

Beatles, The 40

Beaton, Cecil 40

Begin, Menachem, Prime Minister of Israel 226

Beit, Alfred 107

Bell, Alexander Graham 78

Benchley, Robert 35

Bergé, Pierre 236

Bernhardt, Sarah 73, 134

Bert, Paul 267

Betjeman, John 65

Bleakley, Horace 260

Bogart, Humphrey and Bacall, Lauren 165, 166

Booth, John Wilkes 20–21

Borges, Jorge Luis 170

Bouvier, Jacqueline 21

Bowlly, Al 83

Brahms, Johannes 134

Briand, Aristide, Prime Minister of France 114

Britten, Benjamin 155

Brooks, Louise 126

Brosnan, Pierce 117
Brougham, Henry, 1st Baron
    Brougham 112
Bruckner, Anton 134
Bulghakov, Mikhail 212, 214
Burton, Richard 14, 73, 79, 88, 100
Bygraves, Max 92
Byron, Lord George Gordon 141

Cabot, Meg 40
Caine, Michael 261
Callas, Maria 174, 190
Campbell Kawānanakoa, Princess
    Abigail of Hawaii 52
Cantor, Eddie 36
Capone, Al 55, 239
Capote, Truman 25, 40, 190, 213
Carnot, Marie Sadi, President of
    France 102
Caro, Julio de 45
Carpaccio, Vittore 190
Carter, Jimmy, President of the United
    States 226
Caruso, Enrico 126, 174, 199
Castro, Fidel 231
Cavalieri, Lina 161
Champlain, Samuel de 28
Chandler, Edmund 254
Chanel, Coco 110
Chaplin, Charlie 126, 165, 264, 271,
    279
Charles, Emperor of Austria and
    Empress Zita 229

Chetwynd-Talbot, Henry, 18th Earl of
    Shrewsbury 60
Chevalier, Maurice 156, 234,264
Chiang Kai-Shek 32, 225
Chirac, Jacques, President of France
    156
Chirico, Giorgio de 99, 174
Christian IX, King of Denmark 133
Christie, Agatha 218, 224
Chulalongkorn, King of Siam 253
Churchill, Winston 11, 13, 32, 110, 165,
    166, 192, 196, 219, 225, 230, 235, 239
Ciano, Count Galeazzo 99
Clarke, General Dudley 239
Clémenceau, Georges, Prime Minister
    of France 111
Clementi, Sir Cecil 278
Clift, Montgomery 32
Cocteau, Jean 111, 161
Cogna, Alma 92
Cohen, Eve 240
Colette 236
Collins, Joan 14
Collins, Wilkie 160
Connery, Sean 79, 114
Connick, Harry Jnr 37
Conrad, Joseph 263
Cooper, Gary 234
Coward, Noël 11, 37, 256, 260, 263, 266
Crane, Dr Frank 58
Cronkite, Walter 261
Crosby, Bing 57
Cunningham, Alfred 270

Curie, Marie 200

Cushing, Peter 58

D'Annunzio, Gabriele 99, 170, 174, 178

Dalí, Salvador 99

Darwin, Charles 173

Davis, Miles 40

Day-Lewis, Cecil 87

Del Monte, Toti 153

Delon, Alain 114

Deng Xiaoping 277

Dexter, Colin 67–8

Diaghilev, Sergei 160-161

Diana, Princess of Wales 112

Dickens, Charles 20–21, 160

Dietrich, Marlene 11, 40, 73, 126, 156, 234

Dolgorukaya, Princess Stephanie 210

Dos Passos, John 208, 217

Dostoyevsky, Fyodor 204

Douglas, Kirk 282

Doyle, Arthur Conan 60, 224

Drobny, Jaroslav 155

Duhamel, Georges 236

Duras, Marguerite 236

Dürer, Albrecht 145

Durrell, Lawrence 240

Duse, Elenora 178

Dutra, Eurico, President of Brazil 46

Dvořák, Antonin 62

Eastwood, Clint 79

Edison, Thomas 126

Edward VII, King of England 59, 64, 70, 106, 107, 109, 122, 222

Edward VIII, King of England, aka Duke of Windsor (with and without Mrs Simpson) 13, 46, 57, 138, 176

Eiffel, Gustave 102

Einstein, Albert 45

Eisenhower, Dwight D. 13, 40, 87

Élisabeth, Duchesse de Clermont Tonnerre 70

Elizabeth II, Queen of England 32, 190

Emerson, Ralph Waldo 20

Ephron, Nora 40

Eugénie, Empress of France 59, 224

Fabergé, Peter Carl 254

Fairbanks, Douglas Jnr 282

Fairbanks, Douglas Snr 36

Fargue, Léon-Paul 96

Farouk I, King of Egypt 225

Farrington, Wallace R., US Governor 52

Faulkner, William 25–6, 36

Fellini, Federico 180

Feydeau, Georges 105

Fitzgerald, Scott and Zelda 39, 110

Fitzgerald, Ella 156

Fonda, Jane 272

Fonteyn, Margot 78

Ford, Henry 126, 176

Forrer, Ludwig, Swiss President 151

Franz Joseph I , Emperor of Austria 130, 138

Fraser, Brendan 261

Freeman-Thomas, Marquess of
  Willingdon 250

Freud, Sigmund 178

Gabor, Zsa Zsa 14

Gandhi, Mohandas 247, 251

Garbo, Greta 40, 165, 181–3

Gardner, Ava 266

Garland, Judy 57

Gaulle, Charles de 32, 165, 236

Gautier, Théophile 204

Gellhorn, Martha 88

George I, King of Greece 134

George II, King of Greece 196

George VI, King of England 46, 224

George, Grand Duke of Saxony 181

Gershwin, Leonore 213

Gilbert, W.S. 69, 72

Giordano, Umberto 174

Goddard, Paulette 271

Godfrey, Howard 83

Goebbels, Joseph 218

Goering, Hermann 110

Gökalp, Mehmed Ziya 217

Gorky, Maxim 214

Grace, Princess of Monaco 32, 114, 117

Grandi, Dino 178

Grant, Cary 40, 117

Grant, Ulysses S. 147

Greene, Graham 139, 165, 219, 260–61

Grey, Effie 163

Grieg, Edvard 199

Grisham, John 26

Gritti, Andrea, Doge of Venice 162

Guggenheim, Peggy 166

Guinness, Alec 78

Guinness, Rupert, 2nd Earl of Iveagh
  191

Gulbenkian, Calouste 107

Hari, Mata 97

Harlow, Jean 264

Harris, Richard 73

Hawthorne, Nathaniel 20

Hawtrey, Charles 73

Hemingway, Ernest 11, 13, 26, 67, 73,
  85, 87, 110, 166, 175, 188, 217

Hemingway, Hadley 175

Hemingway, Mary 26

Hemingway, Pauline 26

Henry, Émile 104

Hitchcock, Alfred 32, 40, 89, 117, 236

Hitler, Adolf 13, 128, 134, 202, 208,
  210, 218

Hồ Chí Minh 21, 271

Holford, Robert Stayner 85

Holmes, Oliver Wendell Snr 20

Howard, Trevor 266

Hugo, Victor 173

Huston, John 231

Hutton, Barbara 190, 256

Huxley, Aldous 244, 246

Hvorostovsky, Dmitri 214

İnönü, Erdal, President of Turkey 218

Isherwood, Christopher 274

Jackson, Michael 129
Jagger, Mick and The Rolling Stones
    166, 214
James, Henry 22
James, Henry Snr 20
Jinnah, Muhammad Ali 246, 247, 251
John, Elton 90, 209
Johnson, Hewlett 212

Kalākaua, King of Hawaii 48
Kamehameha V, King of Hawaii 49
Kathpurthala, Maharajah of 246
Kaufman, George S. 35
Kaye, Danny 13
Kennedy, John F., President of the
    United States 21
Kerr, Deborah 89
Kidman, Nicole 166
King, Mackenzie, Prime Minister of
    Canada 32
Kipling, Rudyard 261
Kitchener, Field Marshal 39
Kleberger, Johannes 145
Klimt, Gustav 131
Kline, Kevin 117
Kossak, Wojciech 202
Kraus, Karl 131, 134

Lancaster, Burt 78
Lancaster, Osbert 67
Lanza di Trabia, Prince Raimondo 180

Larkin, Philip 68
Laurel, Stan and Hardy, Oliver 79
Lean, David 89
Lempicka, Tamara de 174
Lenin, Vladimir 212
Lennon, John and Cynthia 89
Lennon, John (see The Beatles) with
    Yoko Ono 139
Leopold I, King of the Bavarians 148
Leopold III, King of the Belgians 153
Lerner and Loewe 37
Lincoln, Abraham 20
Liszt, Franz 148
Lloyd-George, David 114
Longfellow, Henry Wadsworth 20
Lonsdale, Stella 83
Luciano, Charles 'Lucky' 57
Ludwig I, King of Bavaria 148
Lutyens, Edwin 91, 249
Lvov, Prince Alexi 209

Mackintosh, Charles Rennie 79
MacLaine, Shirley 282
MacMahon, Patrice de, President of
    France 133
Mahler, Gustav 131, 134
Majorelle, Jacques 232
Malraux, André 259
Mamoun, Prince of Morocco 232
Mandela, Nelson 78, 89
Mann, Thomas 126
Manning, Olivia 239
Mao Zedung 277

Maple, Blundell 242

Marnier-Lapostolle, Alexandre 109

Marx, Harpo 35

Mastroianni, Marcello 214

Maugham, W. Somerset 87, 165, 166, 237, 244, 256, 263, 278

Maxwell, Elsa 109

Mayréna, Marie-Charles David de, King of the Sedang 259

McCartney, Paul 209

Melba, Nellie 107

Menuhin, Yehudi 155

Messel, Oliver 88

Metaxas, Ioannis, Prime Minister of Greece 195

Millais, John Everett 163

Miller, Arthur 40

Mills, Hayley 266

Milne, General George 214

Minnelli, Liza 40

Miranda, Carmen 47

Mitterrand, François, President of France 32

Mix, Tom 36

Modugno, Domenico 180

Mohamed ben Abdallah, King of Morocco 232

Mohammed Shah, Aga Khan III 190

Monet, Claude 104

Monroe, Marilyn 40

Montez, Lola 148

Montgomery, General Bernard 178, 226, 239

Moore, Roger 14, 156

Morecambe, Eric 90

Morgan, Michèle 235

Moscicki, Ignacy, President of Poland 202

Mountbatten, Lord Louis 246, 249

Munnings, Alfred 87

Murrow, Ed 62

Mussolini, Benito 114, 134

Nani Mocenigo, Contessa Amalia 190

Napoleon III, Emperor of France 101

Napoleon, Prince Jérôme, 'Plon Plon' 160

Neeson, Liam 124

Nehru, Jawaharlal 247, 251

Nicholson, Jack 214

Nicolson, Harold 110

Nietzsche, Friedrich 173

Nixon, Tricia 40

Nobel, Alfred 150

Nureyev, Rudolf 174

O'Toole, Peter 282

Offenbach, Jacques 20, 22

Olga, Grand Duchess of Russia 178

Olivier, Laurence 36, 92, 77

Onassis, Aristotle 190

Oppenheimer, George 35

Osborne, John 92

Oscar II, King of Sweden 147

Otéro, Caroline 114

Pacino, Al 166

Paderewski, Ignacy 198–200

Paolo, Prince of Serbia 178

Parker, Dorothy 35–8

Parker, Sarah Jessica 236

Pascal, Gabriel 89

Paul, Henri 112

Paul, Howard 60

Pavarotti, Luciano 209

Peck, Gregory 231

Pedro II, Emperor of Brazil 133, 173

Pemberton, Max 29

Pessoa, João, President of Brazil 43

Philip, Duke of Edinburgh 32, 190

Philip, Prince of Württemberg 131

Piaf, Edith 234

Picasso, Pablo and Khokhlova, Olga 161

Pickering, Harry 187

Pickford, Mary 110

Pius V, Pope 158

Porter, Cole 110

Priestley, J.B. 63

Proust, Marcel 110–11

Pym, Barbara 68

Raffles, Sir Stamford 262

Rama VI, King of Siam 254

Rasputin, Grigory 210

Ravel, Maurice 236

Reagan, Ronald 32

Reed, John 212

Rendell, George 219

Rice, Anne 26

Rilke, Rainer Maria 134

Rinder, Max 229

Rio, Dolores del 48

Rockefeller, John D. 126

Rodolfo Boncompagni Ludovisi, Prince of Piombino 177

Rogers, Ginger 57

Rogers, Roy and Trigger 78

Romanoff, Grand Duke Michael Alexandrovich 116

Romanoff, Grand Duke Michael Mikhailovich 112

Romanoff, Grand Duke Nikolay 114

Romanoff, Grand Duke Peter 114

Romanoff, Tsar Nicholas II 77, 116, 126, 253

Romanoff, Tsar Peter I 204

Rommel, Erwin 13, 178, 239

Roosevelt, Franklin D. 32, 52, 100, 225, 235

Ross, Harold 37

Rostropovich, Mstislav 214

Rothschild, Mimi Franchetti 185

Rufini, Cavalier 176

Ruskin, John 65, 163, 166

Ryabushinsky, Dmitry 207

Ryan, Meg 117

Sacher, Franz 136

Sadat, President Anwar 226

Sakai, General Takashi 279

Salote, Queen of Tonga 79

Sargent, Malcolm 78

Sassoon, David 277–8

Schulz, Dutch 57

Scott, Captain Robert 227

Scott, Colonel Robert Lee Jnr 281

Scott, Sir Walter 78

Shackleton, Ernest 227

Shah, Mohammed Zahir, King of
   Afghanistan 153

Shaw, George Bernard 73, 208, 212,
   229

Shelley, Percy Bysshe and
   Wollstonecraft, Mary 141, 146

Sherwood, Robert E. 25

Sibson, Dr Francis 144

Sica, Vittorio de 174

Singh, Maharajah Bupinder of Patiala
   126, 251

Sissi, Empress Elisabeth of Austria
   138, 227

Smolka, Peter 139

Souidan, Dr Zaki 225

Springsteen, Bruce 166

St Laurent, Yves 236

Stalin, Josef 40, 212, 225

Stalin, Svetlana 40

Stanley, Edward George Villiers, Earl
   of Derby 91

Stevenson, Robert Louis 49, 78

Stewart, James 236

Stoddart, Joseph Marshall 60

Strauss, Johann II 131

Strauss, Richard 199

Stravinsky, Igor 161, 165

Sullivan, Arthur 69

Taylor, Elizabeth 13, 73, 79, 88, 100,
   156, 266, 282

Tchaikovsky, Peter Ilych 97, 168, 170,
   207

Teresa, Princess of Bavaria 178

Thompson, Emma 117

Thompson, Kay 40

Thurman, Uma 114

Torlonia, Count Giovanni 157, 158

Trinder, Tommy 92

Turgenev, Ivan 204–05

Turner, J.M.W. 157

Twain, Mark 20, 60, 121

Umberto II, King of Italy 231

Valentino, Rudolf 110

Valéry, Paul 236

Vanderbilt, George 55

Venizelos, Eleftherios 195

Verdi, Giuseppe 174

Vittorio Emanuele II, King of Italy 170

Victoria, Queen of England 97

Visconti, Luchino 174

Von Bismarck, Otto 133

Von Choltitz, Dietrich 99–100

Von Hindenburg, Paul 184

Von Kurowsky, Agnes 175

Von Meck, Nadezhda 97

Von Metternich, Prince Klemens 136

Von Papen, Franz 178

Von Sternberg, Josef 234

Von Stroheim, Eric 235

Von Suttner, Bertha 150

Wagner, Richard 134, 147–8, 173

Waldorf, William Astor 82, 242

Wałęsa, Lech 203

Walsh, Thomas 'Fatty' 57

Waugh, Evelyn 68

Weiderhorn, Ken 58

Weissmuller, Johnny 58

Welles, Orson 48, 139, 165, 190, 231

Wells, H.G. 208, 212

Wells, Rebecca 26

Welty, Eudora 26, 27

Wesendonck, Otto and Mathilde
  147–8, 151

Wharton, Edith 21

Wilde, Oscar 60

Wilder, Thornton 36

Wilhelm II, German Emperor 124, 151

Williams, Tennessee 25, 26–7

Winslet, Kate 166

Wood, Edward, 1st Earl of Halifax 87

Woollcott, Alexander 35, 38

Woolworth, Edna 39

Woolworth, Jessie 39

Wright, Frank Lloyd 15, 165

Wulfert, Natalia Countess Brasova 116

Wyler, William 40

X, Malcolm 21

Young, Sir Mark Aichison 279, 281

Yussupov, Prince and Princess 161

Zhang Chunquiao 277

Zog, King of Albania 225

BEHIND THE SCENES

An index of hoteliers and general managers, chefs and bar staff, and of architects, designers and decorative artists who made it all possible.

Adlon, Lorenz 124–7

Adlon, Louis 126–7

Andersen, Andersen and Kinch 252–3

Auzello, Claude 110

Baur, Johannes 146–7

Baur, Theodor 147–50

Beinecke, Bernhard 39

Bengalia, Arthur 52

Bidwell, R.A.J., architect 262

Bieger, Felix 282

Black, Harry S. 39

Blandy family 229, 230

Blomfield, Charles G., architect 249

Bodne, Ben and Mary 36, 37

Bodosakis, Prodromos 217

Bolkiah, Hassanal, Sultan of Brunei 180

Bowman, John McEntee 54–7

Bujault, Madame M.O. 254

Carnevali, Nicola, architect 157

Carte, Bridget D'Oyly 69

Carte, Helen 68, 72

Carte, Richard D'Oyly 68–74, 107

Carte, Rupert D'Oyly 68, 72, 73

Caruthers, Philip 47

Case, Frank 33–8

Cazeau, Pierre 257

Chambers W.A., architect 243

Chewning, Chuck, designer 166

Ciaceri, Gianfrancesco 178

Cipriani, Arigo 188, 190

Cipriani, Giuseppe 186–91

Clarke, George Somers, architect 227

Coleman, Ada 'Coley' 73

Collcutt, Thomas Edward, architect 70

Craddock, Harry 73

Dabescat, Olivier 111

Dalmas, Charles, architect 113

De Santis, Valentina 186

Deroy, Fred 155

Doherty, Henry Latham 57

Dorn, Marion, artist 91, 94

Ducamp, André 269, 270

Ducrot, Vittorio, designer 183

Dufour, Guillaume-Henri, designer 143

Dumoutier, Gustave-Emile 267–70

Emerson, Dr Charles 262

Escoffier, Auguste 70–72, 113, 121

Ferdinand, Duc de Montpensier 259

Ferrario, Constantino, architect 183

Forte, Sir Charles 84

Forte, Sir Rocco 162, 213

Foster, Albert 33, 36

Francini, Mathieu 259

Francini, Philippe 260

Frohner, Johann 134

Gaddi, Leo 281

Gandola, Ernea and Maria 181–6

Gandolfo, Luigi 229

Garcia, Jacques, designer 236

Garioch, Billy 78, 79

Giles, John, architect 59

Gill, Eric, artist 91, 94

Gire, Joseph, architect 45, 47

Gottlob, Georges 121

Grosstephan, Charles 259

Guinle, Octavio 43–7

Gurtler, Hans, Poldi and family 138–40

Hardenbergh, Henry J., architect 38, 39

Hassler, Albert 177

Hassler, Berta 177

Herrmann, Julius and Josef, designers 195

Hill, Oliver, architect 90, 92

Hillengass, Otto and Ferdinand 121

Hilton, Conrad 42

Holtman, Franka 100

Hurst, Franklin 'Bill' 253

James, Sandy 77

Jinnah, Ratanbai Petit 244

Kadoorie, Sir Elias and Sir Eleazer 278–9

Kadoorie, Sir Horace 281

Kadoorie, Sir Michael 282

Kahn, Otto 121

Kaufmann, Freddy 274

Kentros, Stavvas 192–3, 197

Kracht, Karl 150

Krull, Germaine 257

Lameire, Charles Joseph, artist 104

Lampsas, Efstathios 192

Laprade, Albert, architect 232

Lavezzari, Emile, architect 232

Lidval, Fyodor, architect 209, 210, 214

Lièvre, Robert, architect 232

Lisch, Jean Juste Gustave, architect 102

Lo Ka Shui 63

Locke-King, Hugh and Ethel 221, 222

Lorizdo, Alessandro, architect 237

Mackenzie, Alexander Marshall, architect 79, 80

Maire, Auguste and Marie 254–6

Marceau, Alphonse 84

Marconi, Władysław, architect 198, 203

Matson, William 49, 50

Maxwell, Edward and William, architects 30

Mayère, Marcellin, architect 114

McAlpine, Sir Robert 85, 87

Merrick, George 54–7

Metzger, Albert 237–41

Metzger, Patricia 241

Meurice, Charles Augustin 96, 106, 143

Miciol, August, architect 143

Micklethwaite, J.T., architect 227

Monteleone, Antonio and family 23–7

Muhayyes, Misbah 218

Muzio, Giovanni, architect 176

Mylius & Bluntschli, architects 118

Nénot, Henri Paul, architect 97

Ngiam Tong Boon 263

Niel, Giuseppe da, 'Danieli' 106, 167

Nistelweck, Francesco 160, 177, 178

Nungovich, George 224

Ornstein, Oscar 47

Pacon, Henri, designer 105

Painter, Walter S., architect 30

Palmer & Turner, architects 273, 274

Parker, Harvey D. 18–22

Pazala, Andrea, architect 171

Peddie & Kinnear, architects 75

Petrakopoulos, Theodoros 193, 195

Plesch, Henry 77

Polizzi, Olga, designer 162

Price, Bruce, architect 28–30

Prost & Marchiso, architects 232

Ravilious, Eric, artist 91, 94

Reid, William 226–7

Reid, William and Alfred 227

Ritz, César 70–72, 97, 106–12, 113, 121, 122

Ritz, Marie-Louise 109, 112

Ritz, Monique 112

Robertson, F.S. 254

Rodakowski, Baron Ernst 222

Roszkowski, Stanisław 198

Roth, William P. 49, 50

Rufenacht, Alexandre 141

Ruhl, Henry 113

Sacher, Anna 136, 138

Sacher, Eduard 106, 135, 136

Sanders, Edward 79

Sanderson, James 60

Sarkies Brothers 262–4

Sassoon, Sir Victor 272–7

Scherz, Andrea and Thierry 15, 156

Scherz, Ernst and Silvia 152–6

Scheurich, Henri-Joseph 97

Schulze & Weaver, architects 54

Schumann, Charles 60

Sherwood, James 47, 191, 220

Singh, R.B.S. Narain 249

Singh, S.B.S. Ranjit 249

Smith, Henry W. 253

Sonnemann, Leopold 118

Sorabji, Khansaheb 243

Spatz, Giuseppe 173, 174

Starck, Ara, artist 100

Starck, Philippe, artist 100

Steffen, Robert 152

Steinberger, Albert 122

Sterry, Fred 39

Stiller, Josef and Anna, 138, 139

Stryjeriski & Mączyński, architects 198

Suave, Joseph 177

Taché, Eugene-Etienne, architect 28

Tata, Dorabji 244

Tata, Jamsetji Nusserwanji 242–7

Tata, Ratanji Dadabhoy 244

Taittinger, Guy 105

Thompson, Jim 257

Tite, Sir William, architect 74

Troisoeufs, George 252

Troller, Teddy 264

Trump, Donald J. 42–3

Trump, Ivana 42

Turrettini, Maurice, architect 145

Valadier, Giuseppe, architect 157, 158

Vallaury, Alexander, architect 215

Vaseli, Romolo 161

Vaterlaus, Ricky 282

Von Landau, Horace 131, 133

Wagner, Otto, designer 198–9

Warren & Wetmore, architects 50

Watson, John 242, 249

Weckel, Emil 222, 224

Wetzlar von Plankstern, Baroness 162

White, Captain James 252

Wilkinson, William, architect 65

Wilson, George Leopold, architect 274

Wolflisberg-Giger, Joseph 205

Zanetti & Adam, architects 121